Clay Shooting

with the

Experts

PAUL BENTLEY

Clay Shooting

with the

Experts

B.T. Batsford Ltd · London

First published 1994

Typeset by Graphicraft Typesetters Ltd.,
Hong Kong
and printed in Great Britain by
Butler and Tanner,
Frome, Somerset
Published by
B.T. Batsford Ltd
4 Fitzhardinge Street
London W1H 0AH

A catalogue record for this book is
available from the British Library

ISBN 0 7134 6910 2

CONTENTS

INTRODUCTION

USING A shotgun to break a few clay saucers might seem a very mundane pastime, and indeed it is if those saucers are propped against a post and are shot at close range. Launch those same clay saucers into the air at speed, though, and suddenly the marksman is presented with a much greater challenge. Now make those same clays fly at various heights and angles, as well as in pairs that sometimes travel in different directions, and you have the makings of a game that really tests hand and eye co-ordination to the limit. This is clay target shooting, and since it requires neither great strength nor a high degree of athleticism, it is a sport that may be practised at a high level by either sex and by people of all ages.

Clay shooting has become very specialized during the past ten years, to the point that a first class performance level in all disciplines is very difficult to achieve – and there are very many disciplines to choose from! Trap alone has five quite distinct disciplines, while one of these, Down the Line, has several sub-disciplines. There are also three Skeet disciplines and two Sporting dis-ciplines. Competition in all is intense, obliging leading shooters to specialize in a particular discipline if they hope to win major events or make their national team. Indeed, in the two Olympic disciplines the participants tend to concentrate on them to the exclusion of all else. Highly successful clay shooting nations like Italy and the Czech Republic take pains to ensure that their international team members stick strictly to their own discipline, and their results in international events suggest they have a point.

In the UK and the USA this kind of discipline segregation, where it occurs, is self-inflicted. It is a strange fact that while Sporting shooters and Skeet shooters will occasionally mix disciplines, they rarely shoot Trap. For their part the Trap shooters tend to stick with their own games, even keeping to their own particular Trap discipline rather than dabbling in several.

Of course, not everyone is interested in being top dog. The great majority of those who shoot clays do so because they enjoy it for its own sake, not because they hope to win a major event. Even among this happy band, however, very few are so uninterested in their results that they will be content to blaze away for years without seeing some improvement. There is a competitor in all of us, however well concealed, and if we are not out to beat the world it is still highly satisfying occasionally to thrash Trevor, Graham and the rest of the lads at the twice-monthly club shoot! Anyone can achieve a decent standard, but only after they have first mastered the basics of good shooting.

When I was a regular competitor on the international ISU Skeet circuit I would spend many, many hours on the practice range, trying to perfect a method of shooting that would hold together under the pressure of a major event like a world or European championship. Frequently I would practise with people who were struggling to shoot even an average score. Usually it was all too obvious that their shooting would always let them down, because their basic shooting method was flawed. It always seemed such a waste of effort when all that was required was something simple like a change in gun mounting or stance to transform the way that person performed. Yet I seldom passed comment, because advice un-sought is seldom accepted gracefully, and usually I had enough problems of my own to think about. Personally I was concerned only with detail: good basic technique was so deeply ingrained that I can honestly say I was never troubled by gun mounting errors, bad balance or poor stance. I was not born with this ability – I had it drummed into me as a boy by my shooting school mentor at Holland & Holland, Norman Clarke. I handled guns all day and every day, and while I might not have shot them as frequently as I handled them I took every opportunity to mount them and swing them correctly, until basic technique was second nature. Few people have such a marvellous opportunity as I did, to work at a shooting school and at an early age to be taken under the wing of one of the best shooting instructors in the world. It did not cost me anything, either!

I firmly believe that if you can ride a bicycle or drive a car then you can also learn to shoot well: but you have to know how. In this book the techniques of leading shooters are examined in detail. Varied though the individual styles may be it should be noted that consistent results are founded on good basic technique. I am confident that many of those struggling to improve will find something within these pages that will set them on the right path to better shooting.

Throughout this book the text refers to the shooter as 'he', rather than endlessly repeating 'he or she', and it also assumes 'he' to be right-handed. No sexism or rightism or any other -ism is intended, it is for simplicity of style and nothing else. Apologies are extended to those who feel sensitive about such things, however.

PART ONE

Choosing the Right Equipment

1

GUNS

T HE DAYS when a shooter used his old and trusty side-by-side pigeon gun for his forays into the clay shooting world have now all but disappeared, at least if the shooter takes his clay shooting seriously. These days clay shooting invariably takes priority, and it is far more likely that the clay shooter will be using his clay gun if and when he shoots live quarry.

GAME AND CLAY GUNS: THE DIFFERENCES

Guns intended for clay shooting are dissimilar in detail to their game shooting counterparts, because they have to satisfy a different set of criteria. The modern game gun has changed very little from the days when huge bags of game were shot. Then the shooter would invariably use two guns and have a man to load them: the idea was to work as a team to get as much shot in the air as possible, hopefully with a high degree of accuracy, too. This required a good understanding between the loader and his man, and fast loading and efficient gun exchanging were the order of the day. The guns that evolved for this task

were light in weight, easy to handle and side-by-side. Low weight was very important, because a heavy gun would soon become very tiring to shoot (and carry) during a long day. The side-by-side configuration is also far quicker to load than the over-and-under, the barrels of which have to drop open further than those of the side-by-side in order to load the two cartridges. With these advantages the side-by-side became the only gun worth considering for game shooting.

Clay shooting makes different demands on a gun, however. Speed of loading is of no consequence, nor is light weight. In fact, game guns are something of a compromise where weight is concerned, being too light to allow the truly precise handling required of the clay gun. So clay guns are built to an ideal shooting weight, with ease of carrying being of secondary importance. Precision shooting is vital in a sport where the difference of one target can separate a world champion from the also-

1 *The over-and-under is the choice of most serious clay shooters*

rans. This is another area where the over-and-under scores over the side-by-side (1). The O/U's narrow barrel/rib profile makes for ready target alignment, or 'pointability' as it has come to be known in clay shooting circles. This word may convey little to the layman but means everything to the clay shooter.

The clay gun

The purpose built clay gun will weigh at least a pound more than the average game gun, a significant percentage increase when you consider that a 12 bore game gun weighs about 6 lb 8 oz. The typical clay gun will be an over-and-under, single trigger, with ventilated top rib and perhaps similar side ribs, too. It will have a full or semi pistol grip rather than the straight hand of the game gun, and full fore-end instead of the game gun's little 'splinter' affair. No one would willingly carry such a gun all day long in the game field, and at a smart game shoot its use could cause raised eyebrows and even engender muttered asides about 'people who use machine guns'! That is as maybe. The fact remains that at clays someone wielding an over-and-under will shoot the pants off anyone of similar ability using a side-by-side (2). It is as simple as that, and explains why side-by-sides are only rarely seen at clay shoots, and never in the hands of anyone hoping to win!

There are several other types of shotgun suitable for clay shooting besides the O/U:

2 Not even a top quality sidelock side-by-side gun, like this Symes & Wright, can compete with the O/U or semi-auto when clay shooting

- Single shot mono barrelled gun
- Single barrel pump action
- Single barrel semi-automatic

All have their uses but without doubt the only type worth considering as an alternative to the O/U is the semi-auto. Of the two types, O/Us far outnumber semi-autos.

The semi-automatic (3)

For certain shooters the semi-auto has several advantages over the O/U. The

3 *Some shooters swear by the semi-auto, like this Beretta 303. Advantages are low recoil and low cost. The single barrel limits choke selection, though*

gas operated mechanism of the semi-auto tends to reduce recoil, important for those susceptible to it, and these guns are generally rather less expensive than their O/U counterparts. Balanced against this are the sometimes dubious reliability of the semi-auto, the choke limitations of its single barrel layout,

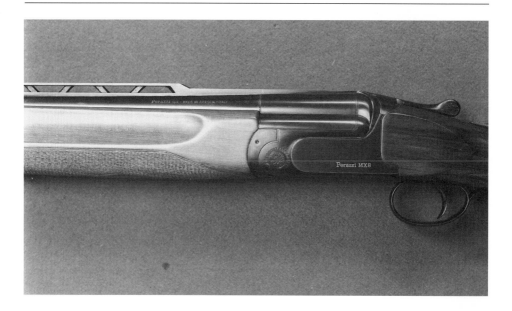

4 *A purpose-built Italian Trap gun: a Perazzi MX8 with raised and ventilated top rib*

and the auto's somewhat utilitarian appearance. Shooters have won world championships with these guns, though, so they are a serious option for those who prefer their features. A number of World ISU Skeet championships have fallen to semi-auto users, Dan Carlisle of the USA being one who also uses his Beretta 303 for Sporting too. Among UK shooters Duncan Lawton, using a Remington auto, has won the FITASC Sporting world championship twice, in 1980 and 1991.

Pump-action gun

Having earlier written off the pump gun it must be said that many American shooters use these guns successfully for ATA Trap. This Trap discipline permits only one shot per target, however, so the inconvenience of having to pump the fore-arm in order to load a second cartridge does not arise. For this purpose the pump gun works very well, and weapons like the Winchester Model 12 are rightly highly regarded.

GUNS FOR DISCIPLINES

Barrel length

Over the years the guns used for the various disciplines have undergone a number of changes. For instance, in the late Seventies the barrel length of a typical Sporting clay gun was 28 in, with some shooters using 26 in barrelled guns. Nowadays an average length is 30 in, with many leading shooters favouring barrels 32 in long. Skeet has seen a similar change: the once favoured 26 in barrels are rarely seen now, with 28 in barrels the norm and with a fair sprinkling of 30 in guns in evidence. Trap shooters have always favoured long barrels, although there are now far more 32 in barrelled Trap guns than there were a few years ago (4).

Rib width

The march of fashion has not been limited to barrel length. The once popular narrow rib is seldom seen now, nor is the extra wide rib once so popular on guns like the Nikko Shadow Indy and the broadway ribbed Browning. Nowadays, ribs tend to be between 10 and 12 mm in width, although some manufacturers offer a tapered rib. The purpose of this is to create the illusion that the barrels are longer than they actually are, the idea being that this should improve pointability. Unfortunately, fitting tapered ribs accurately is extremely difficult. Many are anything but straight, a condition hardly likely to favour accurate shooting.

Weight

Clay shooters have also moved away from relatively light guns, favouring something heavier than was the case five years ago. Whereas $7\frac{1}{2}$ lb was once considered a standard weight for guns of all disciplines the average has now risen nearer to 8 lb.

The rule change which reduced shot loads to 28 g caused a brief ripple of enthusiasm among the gun manufacturers, who saw it as an opportunity to offer lightweight models to suit the lower recoil of the new shells. Unfortunately they had perhaps overlooked that clay guns had grown gradually heavier over the years, not to counter recoil but to match the dictates of good handling and control. The ISU has now reduced the shot charge for its disciplines to 24 g, but it is unlikely that shooters will want lighter guns to match the negligible recoil of such ammunition.

CHOKES

The choke is the bore constriction near the muzzle of practically all modern shotgun barrels, and the importance of choke is such that whole chapters of some shooting books have been devoted to it. Its purpose is to regulate the degree to which the shot spreads after it leaves the barrel. W. W. Greener, while not the inventor of choke, was certainly the gunmaker who developed the choke system and strongly extolled its virtues. Before the advent of choke, shooters had to be content with a relatively short effective range for their guns. This was because the pellets spread rapidly and the pattern soon became full of holes and ineffective.

An early mistake with choke was that shooters and gunmakers confused the issue. Here was a method whereby guns could be made to throw tighter patterns, thus extending the shotgun's range, and everyone wanted barrels to throw patterns as tight as possible in order to extend range to the maximum. This was fine in theory, but many shooters found that their cartridge/ kill ratio got worse instead of better. This was because the new tight patterns put greater demands on shooters' accuracy, so while they gained an extra few yards of range they sacrificed pattern width and missed birds they might otherwise have killed.

Eventually it dawned that at close ranges the tight choke was absolutely the wrong choice, and gradually a set of intermediate chokes sizes were developed. With Cylinder and Full being at the opposite ends of the choke scale (Cylinder throwing the more open

5 *Simple mechanics and coil mainsprings give the O/U essential reliability for clay shooting*

patterns) the intermediate chokes are:

- Improved cylinder
- $\frac{1}{4}$ choke
- Modified choke
- $\frac{1}{2}$ choke
- $\frac{3}{4}$ choke

In the USA Modified choke falls midway between $\frac{1}{2}$ and $\frac{3}{4}$ choke, while there is also an Extra Full choke which is seldom seen.

Determining choke

Choke is determined in two quite distinct ways, one theoretical, the other practical. The former is arrived at by micrometer measurement of the difference between the barrel bore and the choke cylinder. These differences are in thousandths of an inch, known in the gun trade as 'points of choke'. Thus a full choke is said to have 40 points of choke (the choke cylinder has a diameter 40 thousandths of an inch less than that of the bore), $\frac{3}{4}$ choke has 30 points of choke, $\frac{1}{2}$ choke 20 points of choke, $\frac{1}{4}$ choke 10 points of choke and improved cylinder about 6 points of choke. These measurements indicate the nominal choke only, and a nominal $\frac{3}{4}$ choke might actually throw a $\frac{1}{2}$ choke pattern or conversely a full choke pattern (or, of course, a $\frac{3}{4}$ choke pattern). Points of choke are therefore only a rough guide to the choke's likely performance.

6 *Top GB Olympic Trap shooter, Peter Croft, in action. He popularized the 32in barrel gun in the UK in his discipline*

7 *Most English and NSSA Skeet shooters use 28in barrel guns. Some use 30in guns, a few 32in. For ISU Skeet 28in barrel guns are almost universal*

The practical way to determine choke is to test the gun for pattern gainst a special steel pattern plate. The percentage of the shot charge that falls within a 30 in circle when the gun is fired at a pattern plate at a range of 40 yd tells you exactly what that choke is. The gun is fired at the whitened plate, a 30 in circle is scribed over the centre of the resulting pattern and the pellets within that circle are counted. If you know the total number of pellets in your shot charge then you can easily work out the percentage, and from that the choke.

The pattern percentages are as follows:

- Full choke   70 per cent
- $\frac{3}{4}$ choke   65 per cent
- $\frac{1}{2}$ choke   60 per cent
- $\frac{1}{4}$ choke   55 per cent
- Imp Cyl   50 per cent
- True Cyl   40 per cent

MORE ON WEIGHT AND BARREL LENGTH

Trap

All Trap shooting involves shooting from a dead start, gun mounted. Lacking the advantage of the moving gun mount so typical of good Sporting and Skeet shooting, it might be expected that the Trap shooter would favour a lightweight, short-barrelled gun. Not so. Even at the lightening fast international Trap disciplines, Automatic Ball Trap, Universal Trap and Olympic Trap, the Trap shooter is concerned not so much with speed of movement as with smoothness and control. Although this smoothness and control must originate with the shooter, who after all

is in sole charge of the gun, the gun itself can help or hinder the shooter in his efforts. The expert Trap shooter will avoid reacting violently as he sees the blurred target leave the trap house or trench. He will wait that fraction of a second necessary to get the target in sharp focus then he will move the gun smoothly after it. To assist this controlled action the gun needs a certain weightiness combined with relatively long barrels for added pointability.

Skeet

Unlike Trap, where targets are all relatively long range, a round of Skeet is comprised of a mixture of medium range targets, short range targets, and very short range targets. Shooting skeet doubles also requires that the gun is swung in exactly opposite directions within a very short space of time. A lightweight gun would seem perfect for the job, but in Skeet, as in all forms of shotgun shooting, control is all important with speed of movement coming a poor second. This again means a fairly weighty gun, though not so hefty as the typical Trap gun, nor should the barrels be too long. Weight should be

8 *32in barrels are popular for Sporting, but many shooters are over-gunned with barrels this length*

around $7\frac{1}{2}$ to 8 lb. Some English and NSSA Skeet shooters use 30 in barrels, but 28 in are best for most shooters (7). The combination of a medium weight gun with medium length barrels allows the moderate speed of movement required combined with control.

ISU Skeet features similar range targets to those of English and NSSA, but much faster. Even so, short barrels are out. Inspecting the guns of the world's

top ISU Skeet shooters will reveal guns that rival the Trap gun for weight. Why should this be, if speed is so necessary? It again comes down to the magic word: control. Swinging a lightweight gun with short barrels is a certain way to get speed, but control goes right out the window. For most men, the ISU Skeet gun should have 28 in barrels and weigh in at least around the $7\frac{3}{4}$ lb mark.

Sporting

Like the game gun, the Sporting gun has to be able to handle anything that appears. Typically in this discipline, targets can be almost out of range or practically on the end of the gun, as well as everything in between. Something similar to a Skeet gun might be thought ideal for the job, and for many years 28 in barrelled guns dominated the Sporting scene. A gun of Skeet gun weight is still about right, but many of the top Sporting competitors have taken to using 32 in barrels, although most Sporting shooters are over-gunned with such weapons. In the right hands 32s are beautiful for sorting out those long crossers, where those extra few inches permit real precision shooting. Where these guns can fall down is on the relatively close targets, and these form 60 per cent of the targets at most shoots. The great Sporting shooters can handle these close targets with their 32s, and then benefit from the 32 in barrels on the long testing targets (8). But Mr Average (and a few of the best Sporting shooters, truth be known) finds the extra length a decided handicap for close work, and scores suffer accordingly. One of the UK's most consistent Sporting

Changing chokes

When A. J. Smith (9) won a world FITASC Sporting championship using no more than $\frac{1}{4}$ and $\frac{1}{4}$ for all the many and various range of targets presented, the proof of the claim seemed established.

However, the truth behind the Smith choke set-up was rather more prosaic than it appeared. The reason his $\frac{1}{4}$ chokes stayed in place throughout the competition was simply that A. J. couldn't move them. Through lack of cleaning they had got firmly stuck and wouldn't budge!

A. J. Smith aside, many leading shooters change their chokes from stand to stand. Former British Open champion, Gary Phillips, strongly believes in changing chokes to suit the target. His Miroku, a converted Trap gun, is fitted with the excellent chokes made by Nigel Teague. Nigel specializes in fitting multichoke tubes to fixed choke guns, and they are extremely slim and light and have no noticable effect on the gun's balance. Gary can be seen changing chokes on almost every stand, and spends much time studying targets before deciding which combination to employ.

9 A. J. Smith in action

competitors, former World champion John Bidwell, still swears by his $27\frac{1}{2}$ in barrelled Browning, which he shoots with great accuracy, and the vast majority of Sporting shooters would be well advised to take him as a role model and forget the long barrel boys.

TIGHT OR OPEN PATTERNS?

Once upon a time buying a gun also meant having to carefully select the chokes at the same time. They were part and parcel of the gun and were fixed during manufacture, and could only be altered following extensive (and expensive) attention from a gunsmith. Many Sporting guns were made with a choke combination such as $\frac{1}{4}$ and $\frac{3}{4}$. This meant that one barrel could handle the close stuff while the other could deal with the targets at longer range. Where this went badly wrong, of course, was on the frequent occasions when the shooter encountered a pair of close or long range targets. In this instance one choke would be wrong for the target. It meant that many Sporting shooters carried two or even three guns, an expensive, not to mention heavy, cure.

The advent of multichokes has solved the problem, giving the shooter the option of any choke combination he needs for a given stand. When they first appeared many shooters scoffed at the multichoke idea, claiming that once the novelty of these chokes wore off shooters would screw in something like $\frac{1}{4}$ and $\frac{1}{2}$ and never touch the chokes again.

It is well worth testing each choke on a pattern plate, just to see what effect the various tubes have at different ranges. It can be quite an eye opener to see what a full choke does at 15 yd, and what a cylinder choke does at 40 yd. The close range full choke can be covered by a dinner plate, putting unnecessary demands on accuracy. At 40 yd range the cylinder choke is no longer an effective pattern, having holes in it big enough for a pheasant to fly through, let alone a clay target. Then try the full choke at 40 yd and the cylinder at fifteen and you will immediately see the sense in matching the choke to the target.

Chokes to suit your discipline

For Skeet the mandatory size 9 shot will give a perfectly adequate pattern with cylinder choke at all Skeet ranges, which should never exceed 25 yd. Pattern test your gun at this range and see for yourself. It's very reassuring.

Chokes for Trap depend on the discipline. For the international Trap games, ABT, U/T and O/T, most shooters opt for $\frac{3}{4}$ or full for the first barrel and full for the second. Second barrels are often taken at 40 yd or more, and at that range with a 24 g shot load you need all the pattern you can get. Strange though it may seem many cartridges intended for specialized second barrel use are actually lower velocity than those intended for first barrel work. This is because lower velocity tends to mean a lower operating pressure, and lower pressure tends to have a tightening effect on the pattern. With a full choke this leads to a pattern a touch tighter than full, just the job on a rapidly receding long range target.

DTL targets are usually shot well

inside 30 yd, at least with the first barrel, yet many leading shooters prefer a similar choke combination to those favoured by international competitors. The main reason for this is the confidence they claim to get from seeing the target 'smoke', although arguably half choke, at least for the first barrel, is quite enough for the job.

The secret of good choke selection is to use no more than is absolutely necessary to ensure a certain kill when the target is caught by the main pattern. To use a tighter choke than is strictly required for a given target is to handicap yourself. If you barely miss a close range target with a full choke pattern you have given the opposition a target that a wider choke would have claimed as a kill. Who can afford to do that?

2

GUN FIT

A NY GUN shop worth the name will have a wonderful selection of guns to choose from; some cheap, some reasonable, some outrageously expensive. Fortunately for the would-be purchaser good shooting is not determined by the price of the gun but by its suitability for the person buying it. Granted good mechanical condition any gun can be made to shoot well simply by ensuring that the gun fits, or is made to fit, its owner.

Shape

The shape of the modern shotgun is the result of an evolution that has taken place over a period of several hundred years, and there are probably few better examples of form following function. Every part of the gun exists in its present form for a good, sound reason. This is not to suggest that each part of a gun must conform exactly in size and shape to that of every other, however, nor that the shotgun is strictly utilitarian. There are differences between one shotgun and another but they are mostly differences of minor detail rather than of basic design. Although racquets that are in-

tended for tennis, squash and badminton are sufficiently different to be immediately identifiable with their respective games, they all conform to the general form recognized as a racquet. So it is with guns. But whereas, for instance, a tall, slim tennis player can effectively use the identical weight and shape of racquet as someone broader and shorter, the same rule does not necessarily apply to guns and shooting. A tall shooter will usually require a longer stock than his shorter counterpart. Depending on facial shape and the positioning of the eyes the stock might need to be higher or lower in relation to the gun's rib, and it might also need setting off to one side or the other. Establishing these dimensions of stock length and shape for an individual shooter is known as gun fitting.

Provided it is mounted properly a fitted gun will point where the shooter expects it to, without his needing to make any compensating adjustment in his technique. There will not be any misalignment in elevation or direction caused by the gun. It will also readily come to the correct place in his shoulder

10 *Italian ISU Skeet team shooter, Andrea Benelli, shoots with a high stocked Beretta*

and against his face, and will feel comfortable in use. The gun, in fact, will become an extension of the shooter himself. He will be free to concentrate on shooting without having to worry about any equipment deficiencies. This is very important, because shooting presents quite enough problems without them being added to by an ill-fitting gun. Ideally, the shooter can forget about his gun and just get on with the job at hand.

Is gun fitting necessary?

If you hand an unfamiliar factory-made gun to a top shooter he will probably perform well with it. Initially he may not shoot to his usual high standard but after a while he will make any necessary adjustments to his gun mount to accommodate the different stock shape and general feel of the gun. In short, he will fit himself to the gun. Whether he will shoot as well with it as he might is debatable, however. Should he subsequently go back to his own gun, or another gun entirely, he will have to unfit himself and refamiliarize himself with the different weapon. This is not a good idea, and few top shooters use guns that have not been adjusted to suit their own particular characteristics. Yet the vast majority of clay shooters handicap themselves by not attending to their gun fit.

WHAT IS A GOOD GUN FIT?

Before getting too involved in the technicalities of gun fit you must examine closely what you want to achieve. This has already been described in general, but here are the factors in more detail:

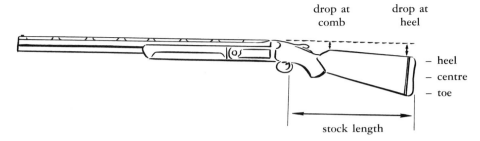

Fig. 1 *Determining stock length and drop*

Stock length

A gun with the correct stock length will come easily to the shoulder (**fig.** 1). It won't get stuck halfway up to the shoulder, nor will it be forced out onto the arm, two of the problems of an over long stock. Short stocks, while easy to mount, are difficult to mount consistently. With a stock that is too long or too short the gun will never feel right, and the shooter will never achieve his potential. Above all, a good stock length will allow full and easy control of the gun at all times.

Bend or drop

This dimension relates the height of the eye relative to the rib. With too little drop the eye is positioned well above the rib, causing the shot to go high. With too much drop the eye is positioned below rib level, a disastrous situation because then you cannot see the target! Of the two errors in gun fit, having too little drop is far better than having too much, but better still is to have it right.

Cast

This dimension relates the eye directionally in relation to the rib (**fig.** 2). Ideally the eye should align exactly over the centre of the rib. If correction is necessary the cast of the stock must be adjusted. Viewed from the rear of the gun, a stock set to the right is said to be cast-off, while one set to the left is said to be cast-on. Generally speaking, right-handed shooters need a degree of cast-off, left handers need cast-on.

It might seem from the foregoing that gun fit could be determined simply by taking certain measurements of the shooter's physique, such as arm length and shoulder width. Unfortunately there are many other factors involved. Muscular development and general flexibility are two that are difficult or impossible

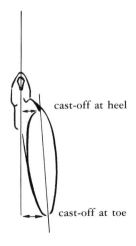

Fig. 2 *Determining the cast-off at heel and toe*

to determine with a tape measure, and to date no one has succeeded in determining all the factors that control gun fit, and it seems unlikely that they ever will. It is largely a matter of trial and error, ultimately arriving at a fit that suits the individual.

ACHIEVING A GOOD GUN FIT

There are two ways to arrive at a good fit. One is to visit a shooting school that has a try gun and an expert with the knowledge to use it properly: the other is to do it yourself.

Using a try gun

A try gun is a gun with an adjustable stock, and the best versions will have adjustments to suit all likely stock dimensions. Unfortunately, despite the very many shooting grounds in the UK, there are relatively few that possess a good try gun and even fewer that employ someone with the necessary expertise to use it properly. In the wrong hands try guns can make a nonsense of gun fit, suffering just as readily as computers do when subjected to the well known 'GIGO' syndrome: Garbage In – Garbage Out! The apparent failure of the computer or the try gun to achieve the desired result lies not with the equipment but the user. In the right hands, though, the try gun is a wonderful piece of equipment that can be used to arrive at a very accurate fit in a relatively short time.

A first class gun fitter will cast his expert eye over his client and adjust the try gun accordingly. After several trial gun mounts and readjustments he will then ask the shooter to fire the gun at a variety of fixed and moving targets, and will make adjustments to the various dimensions according to what he sees. His initial concern will be to get the gun 'looking' right as the shooter handles and fires it. Is it mounting easily? Is the shooter making small but unwanted corrections to his gun mount or his head position in order to accomodate certain slight errors that he may not even be aware of? Does it look, and more important, feel comfortable?

The determination of much of this comes down to the experience and skill of the gun fitter. Once he is satisfied with the way the gun looks he will turn to the next phase, which is making the gun shoot where the shooter is looking.

Adjusting the cast and drop, which respectively determine direction and elevation, is first of all done by shooting at stationery targets. This tells some of the story but not all of it, and a gun that is apparently right when used on a fixed target will usually need minor adjustments when shot at targets that are moving. Eventually the gun fitter will be satisfied with his work, and it is then a simple matter to measure the try gun and prepare a set of dimensions. The shooter's gun can then be altered accordingly.

Fitting a gun yourself

The second method for achieving a good fit is to do it for yourself, although it must be said that this requires no little effort and will take considerably more time than if the job is done by a professional. There are a number of dis-

Making your gun fit you

If you ask several leading shooters how their gun relates to their eye you might well get varying answers. One might like to look flat down the rib. This means that with the gun properly mounted his eye is flat and level with the top of the rib. On a target flying low and directly away from him the target will be partially obscured by the bead. Many Sporting and Skeet shooters use guns like this, but few Trap shooters. John Bidwell is a good example of a top Sporting shooter who prefers this configuration. A gun like this is said to be flat shooting. Another shooter will prefer to look over the rib, so that his eye is positioned slightly above it. On the same low flying going away target he will see the target sitting just above the rib. Most Trap shooters prefer this configuration, and many Skeet and Sporting

shooters favour it, too. Leading Trap shooter Kevin Gill is one who shoots this type of gun. His gun is stocked very high, much higher than most people would be able to handle, yet his results speak for themselves. A gun like this is said to be high shooting. Neither configuration is right or wrong provided it suits the shooter.

What all will be agreed upon, however, is that the eye must be able to look dead straight along the rib, and not be off set to one side or the other. The way to check this is to mount the gun properly with the eyes closed. Open them, and if the eye is not looking exactly down the rib then the gun will always point off line, however slightly. Unless the gun is altered deliberate head movement will be necessary to compensate, and this introduces a variable you can do without.

advantages to this approach. For a start you will not have access to a try gun, and even if you do you probably won't know what to do with it. Remember that a try gun can be a fickle tool in inexperienced hands. Also you will not have an expert watching over your efforts.

Having said that, it must be admitted that the majority of leading shooters in all disciplines do work out their own gun fit, and most feel this to be an important point in gaining confidence in their overall shooting ability. Their results speak for themselves.

ADJUSTING STOCK LENGTH

This measurement is always the first to check and adjust if necessary, since a wrong stock length, particularly an over-long stock, affects the other two main measurements. To determine if your stock is a good length do the following. Take the gun in your right hand, bend your arm to a right angle and then place the butt of the stock in the crook thus formed. If the stock is about the right length then you will be able effortlessly to reach the trigger with the pad and first joint of the index finger. If you cannot reach it, perhaps only stretching to the rear of the trigger guard, then the stock is too long. If you can wrap your finger right around the trigger, perhaps even reaching the front of the trigger guard, then the stock is too short.

To roughly adjust an over-long stock remove the butt plate and any spacers and retry the stock length test. Tape spacers into position until the stock is right. Measure the resulting stock length and have the stock altered professionally. To adjust a short stock simply tape packing to the butt plate until the stock is right, then have it lengthened to that measurement.

Stock measurement

The stock length is always determined as being the length from the middle of the trigger to the centre of the butt. There are two more length measurements, though: the length at heel and the length at toe. On most game guns the length at heel is $\frac{1}{8}$ in longer than the length at centre, while the length at toe is $\frac{3}{8}$ in longer. These dimensions give the familiar concave contour to the butt, designed to fit nicely around the shoulder. There are occasions when it can be a good idea to deviate from these contour dimensions, however. From the point of view of comfort women will often benefit from have the toe measurement reduced by as much as $\frac{1}{4}$ in, and the toe rounded instead of pointed. Shooters who are troubled by the gun slipping down their shoulder as they fire can reverse the toe and heel measurements to give a very slanted butt shape.

This is particularly popular with some Russian ISU Skeet shooters, who take this slant to its limits.

One perhaps obvious point regarding stock length is clothing. It is important to wear the same clay shooting attire at all times, because adding a thick sweater can make a perfect stock feel long. Since most important clay events take place in the warmer months it's as well to fit the gun to suit the type of clothing you wear in these conditions. An alternative is to have several spacers under the butt plate than can be removed when the weather gets cooler and you begin to add the extra layers.

ADJUSTING THE DROP

The drop measurement is taken at two points: at the comb and at the heel. By extending the line of the rib back over the stock these dimensions can be measured in inches. There is no right or wrong drop measurement. Drop at heel, for instance, can be as much as $2\frac{1}{2}$ in or as little as $1\frac{1}{2}$ in (even less for some Trap guns). It all depends on the shooter.

Determining what your personal drop requirement is means firing the gun at a pattern plate at 30 yd (**fig. 3**). Make a mark on the plate, then mount the gun onto it and fire instinctively without attempting to align the gun carefully with the mark. Take several shots to eliminate any accidental misalignments. If two thirds of the pattern are above the mark then the drop is about right. If the pattern is centered on the mark then the drop is too low, and if the pattern is all or nearly all above the mark then the drop is too high. If too low then strips of leather or card can

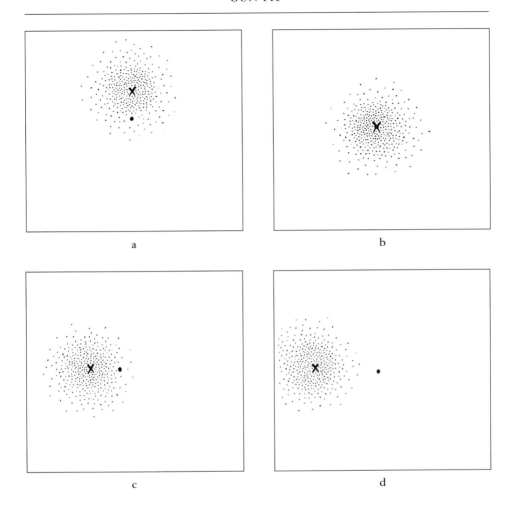

a

b

c

d

be gradually added to the comb of the stock until the gun shoots in the right place. The stock can be altered to this measurement by a gunsmith. If the gun shoots too high then the comb of the stock must be shaved down until again the drop is correct. Care is needed here because even shaving off $\frac{1}{4}$ in can make a lot of difference to the point of impact.

To add complication to the procedure it should be noted that drop is measured at two points along the top of the stock: at the comb and at the heel. Usually the measurement at comb is less

Fig. 3 *Pattern plates shot at 30 yd: (a) pattern $\frac{2}{3}$ above aiming mark – good, (b) pattern dead on – too low; (c) pattern slightly left – cast off to correct, (d) pattern missing well left – close left eye to correct*

than that at heel. Then reason for this slight up slope is to help maintain the face in the right spot on the stock. Reversing the dimensions, for instance, would cause the face to slide down the stock during recoil, and this is not a good idea. The position the face occupies on the stock is crucial to the drop measurement. With a given stock dimension two shooters might have quite different sight pictures. Someone whose face is positioned well up the stock will be further up the slope of the stock, and therefore will see more of the rib than a shooter who keeps his head well back. Once the drop is determined it is important that the face always beds against it at the same spot.

ADJUSTING THE CAST

This can be checked at the same time as the drop is being tested. If everything is as it should be the shot pattern will be dead straight on the mark, although it might also be high or low. Right-handed shooters very seldom shoot to the right of the mark with a factory stock, but some will shoot a touch to the left. This can be corrected by shaving away small amounts of wood from the face of the stock (the place where your face touches the wood) until the gun shoots straight. Large deviations from dead straight (missing the mark completely with all the pattern) are more likely to be caused by a master eye problem, not the gun.

THE MASTER EYE

'You must shoot with both eyes open!' Not so many years ago it was considered sacrilege to suggest that someone should shoot with an eye closed. There is no way of knowing how many shooters have been doomed to poor shooting by this supposed hard and fast rule, but it is a sure bet that over the years it adds up to very many thousands. Much better is to say: 'Shoot with both eyes open if you can – you see better – but don't worry if you can't!' Let me explain this. When shooting a shotgun, there is no sight with which to align the gun with the target, nor is one desirable. The right eye sees the target – the gun is mounted and if everything is right the gun will point exactly where the eye is looking. In effect the eye acts like the backsight on a rifle. To shoot with both eyes open it is essential that the right eye is totally dominant, so that it and it alone dictates the alignment of the gun. Problems arise when the left eye decides it too would like to align the gun. The effect the left eye has is to draw the gun to the left of the target to a greater or lesser degree. Should the left eye be totally dominant then the gun will point several feet to the left of the mark at 30 yd. The shooter thus affected will be quite unaware of this fact unless someone points it out to him, and it is no wonder that he has trouble with his shooting. The problem will not affect him only on straight targets, he will be to the left of everything. This means he will shoot well behind targets travelling left to right, and well in front of those heading in the opposite direction. With all that built-in lead he may well pull off some extraordinary shots at very long range, left crossing targets, but for the most part his shooting will be mediocre.

Determining the master eye

Discovering the master eye is something that should be done right at the beginning of a shotgun shooting career, not several months or years later. Discovering which eye is dominant is simple:

just follow the instructions below.

1 Cut a 1 in diameter hole in a piece of 6 in square card.
2 Look at a spot in the distance and then raise the card so that it interposes between your eyes and the selected spot.
3 Move the card around until you can see the spot through the hole.
4 Close one eye, and if you can still see your spot in the distance then the eye that remains open is the dominant.
5 If all you can see is the card then do the experiment again, but this time close the other eye. Now you can see the spot and the open eye is the dominant one. If you are right-handed then hopefully the dominant eye will be your right eye, since this is the eye with which the gun must align if you are going to shoot with two eyes open.

It is time for further experiment – for this you need the whitened steel pattern plate.

6 Make a mark and shoot at it, both eyes open – make sure the shot is instinctive, with no attempt at deliberate aiming.
7 If when you tried the hole-in-the-card experiment you discovered that your right eye was dominant, this should confirm it. The shot should hit the mark dead straight – any minor horizontal deviation can be corrected by adjustments to the stock.

If the card experiment revealed that your left eye is dominant then shooting at the mark will almost certainly mean a miss or near miss to the left. To con-firm that this is caused by your eye and not some problem with the stock, take a shot with your left eye closed. Once again make it completely instinctive and shoot as the gun comes to the shoulder. The shot should now hit dead on.

Anyone who has been trying to shoot from one shoulder with the opposite eye dominant will know the true meaning of misery! Nothing seems to work, and while both eyes are open nothing *will* work. Close the offending eye and see the difference it makes. Are you bound to shoot poorly with an eye closed? No: some of the finest shots in the world shoot this way, and yet they would be very average shots indeed if they tried to shoot with two eyes open. World and double Olympic champion Luciano Giovanetti of Italy is a one eye shooter. Shoot with two eyes open if you can – after all, you will see better. But if there is any doubt, close the offending eye.

As with so many aspects of shooting, the question of eye dominance is not always quite so cut and dried as we might wish. For instance some people cannot shut one eye without the other closing too. For them it might be possible to learn to shoot from the opposite shoulder, but this will only work if that eye is totally dominant. If the two eyes are sharing the work then the shooter will find that having changed shoulders, instead of missing the target to the left they are now missing it to the right! One idea is to wear an eye patch, another is to fit some sort of vision blocker on the side of the gun. Both are poor solutions to the problem, and much better is to learn to close the eye.

WHEN TO CLOSE THE EYE

The reason that wearing a patch is such a bad idea is because it robs the shooter of binocular vision. Assuming you close an eye then the next question is: when? The answer: as you start moving the gun to the target. At that point your binocular vision will have assessed the target. Close the eye as you start moving and immediately your gun will get onto the right track. It has been suggested by many people who should know better that it is possible to wink the eye shut just before the shot is fired. This is rubbish, because the gun will be off track, thanks to the effect of the dominant eye. Shutting the eye at the last moment will simply let the shooter know that his gun is pointing to the side of the target, but by that time it will be too late to do anything about it. Close the eye early and don't give yourself any nasty last minute surprises. Remember:

• Eye dominance cannot be altered by wearing any form of corrective lens

Also:

• Dominance is not determined by optical strength – the supposedly weaker eye can be the dominant eye
• Most boys and women must shoot with an eye closed
• Most boys after puberty find that they can shoot with two eyes open
• Most men can shoot with two eyes open
• After 45–50 some men find that eye dominance becomes less certain

If you have shot all your life with two eyes open, and suddenly your shooting begins to deteriorate, test them for dominance. They may have begun to change. Some people find that eye dominance changes from day to day, or if they get tired. Some shooters can change eye dominance almost from shot to shot. Any inconsistency in eye dominance has to be eliminated. Do not hesitate: close the eye.

3

CARTRIDGES

THE IDEAL CARTRIDGE?

A GOOD SHOTGUN cartridge can be defined as one that throws a well distributed pattern, is relatively fast, has acceptable recoil and, above all, performs consistently. The arrival of the plastic cartridge case, and with it the plastic wad, represented the first big step forward in shotgun cartridge technology since nitro-based powders replaced the old black powder. The plastic case and wad together allowed a consistency of performance that previously had been impossible with the old paper case and fibre wad. The fibre wad, of uncertain density and construction, was prone to disintegration during its passage through the barrel. This had dire effects on pattern quality. The more expensive, greased felt wad was better than the fibre but still far from perfect. The modern plastic cup wad not only guarantees a near perfect seal for the expanding gasses, it also keeps the pellets from distortion caused by friction with the barrel walls. Bad patterns from plastic wadded cartridges are nowadays very unusual.

The drawback with plastic is an environmental one. When the new plastic cases arrived on the scene it soon became obvious that the disposal of spent cartridge cases could no longer be left to wind and rain. Paper cases soon rotted away, yet the plastic cases remained where they fell until someone picked them up. Correcting this was simple: not so the problem of the plastic wads. For obvious reasons these cannot be picked up: any shoot will distribute thousands of them over a large area. Unfortunately they are a poor addition to a ruminant's diet, and they are also unsightly in sensitive areas.

As a result an increasing number of shoots demand the use of cartridges loaded with fibre wads. This has brought back into focus all the old problems associated with this material. Early attempts to load plastic cases with fibre wads often turned out to be the worst of both worlds. A solution was the use of the plastic over-powder obturator, a small plastic disc with a concave face loaded beneath the fibre wad. This creates an effective seal that no fibre wad used on its own can rival, while the small size of the disc renders it harmless to animals. At the time of writing cartridges loaded with plastic cup wads still considerably outnumber those loaded with fibre, but the ratio is changing.

THE SEARCH FOR VELOCITY

It might be thought that the faster the pellets can reach the target the better, but there are many other related factors that are also important. There is only one way that greater pellet speed may be generated for a given shot load: by applying more push from the rear. This extra 'go' can mean higher breach pressures, increased recoil, and inconsistent patterns. The latter applies particularly to fibre wadded cartridges. None of these three is worth risking for the sake of extra pellet speed. If breach pressures are too high then the gun is at risk. If recoil is high then the shooter's comfort and performance are at risk. If pattern quality suffers then accurately centred targets can escape untouched. Generally speaking the cartridge that performs best on all fronts is seldom the fastest. High speed should never be the criterion by which a cartridge is judged, although some manufacturers make it a selling point.

PATTERN QUALITY

A good pattern is one that, placed with reasonable accuracy and at sensible range, guarantees a broken target. Chokes control pattern density but it is the cartridge itself that determines whether or not the pattern is evenly distributed. The more stable each pellet is as it emerges from the barrel the more true it will fly. A badly spinning or distorted pellet will veer in flight and can be lost to the main pattern. The plastic cup wad prevents pellets abrading against the barrel wall, an action that both spins and distorts the pellet. Further assistance is afforded to pattern quality if the pellets themselves are perfectly round in the first place, and hard. Hardness is achieved by adding antimony to the lead. An antimony content of 5 per cent adds considerably to the crush value of a pellet, without noticably affecting its density. In certain expensive cartridges this hardness and consistency theme is taken further still by plating the shot with copper or nickel. These are mostly used for the international Trap disciplines, where tight consistent patterns at long ranges are the order of the day, although some of the more expensive Sporting cartridges also utilize this type of shot.

SHOT SIZES

Shot sizes for serious clay shooting range from British size 7 through to British size 9, with 7s the larger. In between are sizes $7\frac{1}{2}$ and 8. For Skeet there is no choice: the rules say size 9 only, the reason being that larger pellets would possibly be dangerous where back-to-back ranges are used. As it happens, 9s are ideal at the short range targets encountered at Skeet, and this means that they will work equally well at the same ranges on a Sporting layout.

Size 8s are very much in vogue among Sporting shots, largely due to the publicity given to some leading shooters who use nothing else. What needs to be born in mind, however, is that many of these shooters use cartridges loaded with Italian size 8s, and these equate to British size $7\frac{1}{2}$. Use a British size 8 and you are actually using a smaller pellet than you think.

Many Sporting shooters carry various shot sizes with them, changing the cartridge to suit the target. This can be confusing. Shot size $7\frac{1}{2}$ is probably the ideal all round pellet size for the shooter who has neither the patience nor the inclination to experiment. $7\frac{1}{2}$s will break every type of target at all ranges, and if all other shot sizes were to vanish off the face of the earth it is unlikely that Sporting scores would suffer.

The Trap shooter is in a similar position to the Sporting shot. Because of the ranges involved 9s are out, though not illegal, but he can sensibly use 8s, $7\frac{1}{2}$s and 7s. Which he chooses is up to him, but 8s are arguably too small for anything but DTL or fast first barrel kills at the international disciplines. As with Sporting, $7\frac{1}{2}$s will fit the bill very nicely for both first and second barrel at all Trap disciplines.

CHOOSING A CARTRIDGE

While it is fair to say that these days you would have to try very hard indeed to buy a really bad cartridge, some are nevertheless definitely better than others. There are a great many makes to choose from, and most manufacturers have a range varying from cheapish to very expensive. With some cartridges twice the price of others there is obviously something going into them that is missing in the cheaper ones. This can be divided into three areas:

- Component quality
- Quality of assembly
- Cosmetics

Only the very best powder, shot, case and wad will be used in the most expensive ammunition, and these are not cheap. Quality control will also be closely monitored for the expensive ammunition, reducing the chances of a sub standard round slipping through. Cosmetic treatment is more difficult to justify. High brass cases and metallic finishes to the case help not at all in the search for the perfect cartridge, but they probably help the shooter psychologically. Certainly they add to the eventual price.

What ought the shooter to buy?

The answer probably lies with his ultimate ambitions, as well as his abilities. For a relative novice to lay out a lot of cash for an expensive cartridge is probably a waste of money. An improvement in technique will reap far greater reward than costly ammunition. But for the accomplished shooter, look-

11 *The Eley Olympic Gold is one of the few cartridges made with a paper case rather than plastic. With nickel and copper plating it is a high performance cartridge – at a price!*

ing for major championship success, cheap ammunition is a poor economy. He should purchase the best he can afford. After all, that extra few pounds spent might just buy the target or two that make the difference between first and second place. At any major shoot inspection of what the top performers are using is unlikely to reveal a cheap cartridge.

STEEL SHOT

With 'green' attitudes very much to the fore these days it is not surprising that lead shot has been put increasingly in the spotlight as a potential threat to the environment. Just how rational the arguments against lead shot may be – we have, after all, been drinking water piped through lead for centuries – there seems little doubt that it will eventually be phased out. A number of possible replacements have been tested in recent times, and the outlook is far less gloomy than it was when steel seemed to be the only logical replacement. Although steel is in plentiful supply and is relatively inexpensive it has serious drawbacks. A steel pellet is far less dense than its lead counterpart, and has to be correspondingly greater in diameter to retain reasonable striking energy. This means that less weight of shot can be contained within the limited capacity of a cartridge case, which in turn means a reduced shot charge. The lighter pellets combined with a reduced load inevitably leads to a less effective cartridge. Steel, being so hard, can cause serious barrel damage unless a plastic cup wad is used. No fibre wads here! If steel were the only alternative then the shotgun would become a less effective weapon, which for clay shooting could spell the end of long range targets.

SHOT CHARGE

Not so many years ago $1\frac{1}{4}$ oz loads were considered standard, and when $1\frac{1}{8}$ oz cartridges became mandatory many shooters, especially Olympic Trap shooters, thought that scores would suffer. Oddly enough the opposite proved true. When $1\frac{1}{8}$ oz was replaced by 1 oz, or 28 g, the same doubts were expressed but again these proved unfounded.

Now 24 g loads have been introduced for international Skeet and Trap, and the same fears have been expressed. This time there could well be justification, because the point must eventually be reached where at the longer ranges there is simply insufficient lead in the air to guarantee a broken target even when it is in the centre of the pattern. When an element of luck is brought in then we are no longer involved in a test of skill.

In conclusion, what should the clay shooter buy, since there are so many different makes on the market? The answer depends on what you hope to achieve. Go for the best (and most expensive) if you are already a first class shot and looking for that little extra help to add the odd target to your score. For the majority of shooters, though, find a cartridge that suits you best.

This will be the one that does not knock you about with high recoil, gives satisfactory performance for your shooting level, and, most of all, suits your pocket!

PART TWO

How to Start

4

SHOOTING METHODS

WATCH A number of top shooters in action and it is easy to imagine that there are very many methods of shooting a shotgun. Some shooters stand tall and straight, others crouch. Some swing fast, others swing slow and easy. Some stand with their feet quite far apart, others stand with their feet close together. Take someone like US Skeet shooter Matt Dryke, whose low squat stance looks almost impossible. Yet that squat is nothing to do with his method of shooting. The squat is a reflection of his style, not his method. Regardless of style quirks, all top shooters use a sound method, or they wouldn't be top shooters. Having a solid foundation for your shooting is very important, because if the basic method is wrong then the chances of becoming a good shot, let alone a great one, are zero.

There are only three creditable shooting methods, all of which have their followers, and each method has its fair share of great shooters. The three methods, in no particular order, are:

• Maintained lead

• Swing through
• Point and swing

You can employ these methods from a variety of stances and at greatly varying speeds. It does not matter: the style may change but the method remains. Various celebrated shooting names have become synonymous with one or the other of these methods, but to use these names will only cause confusion. So let us ignore the Stanbury Method, the Churchill Method, the Ruffer Method (Churchill's Method rehashed), the CPSA Method, the Smoke Trail Method and any other methods that might have been ommitted from the list. Regardless of the names, all are one of the three methods first presented.

THE NEED FOR A METHOD

Why bother having a method, and what is method anyway? This question was posed in all seriousness by a very fine Sporting shooter who had been shooting all his life and had never given a moment's thought to technique, or method. Yet his method is excellent, he shoots good scores consistently, and he always features high in the prize lists at any Sporting shoots he attends. But how is this possible, if method is so important? In his formative years this shooter had learned, or more correctly, had absorbed, good technique by watching others who shot properly. The very young will often learn best by following a good example, and in this fashion this top shooter had learned how to shoot without having to consciously apply himself to the task of learning. Thus was born another so-called natural shot, who in fact was no such thing, since he had received the very best education it is possible to have.

Unfortunately few newcomers to the sport have the opportunity to start shooting before or during their early teens. They seldom have the good fortune to have a number of good shots as their unwitting teachers, either. Most people take up clay shooting in their twenties or later, when they are at last in the happy position to afford gun and cartridges and the time to use them. Learning to shoot at this age is like learning to play any game that tests coordination, whether it be golf, or squash, or snooker. It requires lots of concentrated effort. You can play a poor to average game by relying on instincts to pull you through, but unless you understand and practise the basics of these (and any other) games you are unlikely to excel at them.

This is where method comes in. A good shooting method does more than just relate the gun to the target, although that is the main intention. It also defines all the factors that go to make this desirable situation possible. In effect, a good method provides a complete shooting package that can be studied, learned and absorbed, and eventually performed almost without thought. The shooter still relies on instinct, but an instinct that has been conditioned by learning and careful practice. This is crucial. A good method is important, but the sooner it can be consigned to the subconscious, the better.

Although there are three different methods there are certain characteristics of good shooting that are common to all three. These are:

- Gun mounting
- Stance
- Balance
- Swing
- Timing

An inconsistent gun mount, or a consistently wrong gun mount, makes proper eye-target alignment difficult or impossible. A good gun mount accurately relates gun, eye and target. A poor stance prevents the shooter from turning properly. He is forced to twist or bend in order to keep the gun moving, and this drags the gun out of position on the target. A good gun mount is then wasted. Good balance is the ability to remain in full control of your weight distribution throughout a shot. A bad stance will often cause loss of balance, and with it the chances of making a good shot. Making a good, smooth swing depends on a number of factors being right, the most important being gun mount, stance and balance.

Timing means one thing: pulling the trigger at the right moment in the swing to connect with the target. These factors are now examined in more detail.

GUN MOUNTING

Give the average person a gun for the first time and they will almost certainly do most or all of the following. They will take a very wide stance, lean backwards, tense up, carefully juggle the stock onto their arm, then raise the barrels, then lower their head and press their cheek hard on to the stock, and then squint along the rib. All these actions are very natural but very wrong, and only a sadist would encourage someone to fire a gun in this position. Examine the photograph of Duane Morley (12). Notice how he stands fairly erect, but not stiffly. His relatively narrow stance allows free movement in all directions, essential when the target can go left or right, high or low. His 'ready to shoot' position is attentive and relaxed, but definitely not casual, and his head is in a natural position, not forced downwards. From this ideal 'ready to shoot' position the gun is brought smoothly up to meet the face, with the barrels pointing towards the target flight line. It is obvious that Duane Morley's eyes are focussed fully on the target and not the gun. There is no obvious bracing or tightening of the muscles either, only sufficient to maintain full control of the

12 *Relaxed concentration. Top Sporting shot, Duane Morley, in a perfect English Sporting ready position: eyes on the target, barrels pointing towards the target line*

gun during the shot. As in figures 4a and 4b the barrels are never allowed to drop from the target line as the stock is being raised.

Practice makes perfect

Without doubt, learning to mount the gun properly is a very unexciting exercise. Banging away at clays is much more fun! Yet it is no exaggeration to state that gun mounting, both the finished position in the shoulder and the way the gun has arrived there, is the basis on which all good shooting is founded. Anyone who hopes to shoot at the highest level must believe this fact from day one of their shooting career, then concentrate on it and practise good gun mounting regularly. This holds true regardless of the discipline. Trap shooters, who call for their targets with their gun already mounted, must still master this basic principle. Any aspiring Trap champion need only ask the leading performers for their opinion: ignore gun mounting basics and you are likely to doom yourself to mediocre shooting.

Gun up or gun down?

Since all Trap targets emerge from the same spot it is an advantage to begin with the gun already in the shoulder. Indeed, anyone starting with the gun dismounted would be handicapping themselves unnecessarily. However, during recent years an increasing number of shooters have adopted the gun up style for their Sporting and Skeet shooting. This forces the shooter to swing from a static and dead position, which might be alright for slow domes-

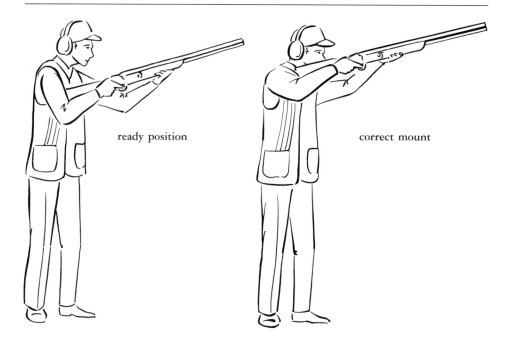

ready position   correct mount

Fig. 4 *Gun mount*

tic Skeet targets (although even that is debatable) but is surely not a good idea at Sporting. At FITASC Sporting the shooter has no choice in the matter since the rules demand the gun is out of the shoulder until the target appears. At English Sporting the rules permit the gun to be mounted prior to the target being called. This is no way to shoot, and observation of the leading shooters will show that none shoots from a ready mounted position. Another drawback with the gun up style is that advancement to FITASC Sporting or ISU Skeet, both enforced gun down disciplines, is made doubly difficult. By all means start with the gun mounted in the early stages of your shooting career, but learn how to mount the gun properly as soon as you can.

STANCE

Good gun mounting relates the gun to the eye and the target but it is correct stance that allows the shooter to use this fact to good advantage, by letting him turn and swing smoothly and in good balance. A good stance also enables the shooter to turn in the right plane, which ensures the gun muzzles stay on the flight line of the target. Points to note are:

- If the shoulders remain square to the target, a good line is maintained without effort. Any stance that prevents this is bad

13 *Left hander, Will Thatcher, staying square to the target as he takes a high left to right crosser*

- Standing with the feet wide apart will prevent the hips from turning, and will force the shoulders to roll over in order to keep the gun moving
- Any form of shoulder rolling will drag the gun off the flight line of the target, with inevitable results
- A very narrow stance will all too easily cause loss of balance, and trying to shoot while falling over is not recommended!
- In a good stance the feet will be no more than shoulder width apart, perhaps slightly less

The actual position of the feet is determined by the target, but generally speaking the leading foot should point slightly to the right of the trap when shooting a straight target, and to a point slightly beyond the place where the target will be shot when taking a crossing target (13).

BALANCE

Remaining in good balance both during and after the shot is vital. Many shooters have to take a corrective step after certain targets, which inevitably means they were losing balance during the shot. This can only lead to inconsistency. Whether the shot was high or low, crossing or quartering, the shooter should afterwards be perfectly able to move immediately and smoothly in another direction if required. Where shooting doubles or second barrels, loss of balance after the first shot probably means the second will be missed:

See it, and shoot it

Peter Croft, one of the UK's most successful Olympic Trap shooters, was once asked to describe his shooting method. He replied: 'I see the target and shoot it.' This answer, which at first seems almost flippant, in fact neatly encapsulates the way a target ought to be shot. See it, swing the gun, shoot it. It is Peter Croft's method of shooting, and that of every other good shot, too. Now examine how Mr Struggling Shooter *thinks* his way through a shot instead of just shooting. It goes something like this: 'Ah, there's the target – now I'll catch it – now I'll swing through it'. All right so far, and just after this the shot should be fired, but the shot is spoiled like this: 'Now I'm ahead of the target – I'll just check the rib to make sure elevation and forward allowance are right – Blast! the target's moved on, I must swing a bit more, now check the rib again – Oh! – better shoot quick before it gets right away from me' – Bang! – missed! There is not enough time to actually hold this sort of conversation with yourself, of course, but many shooters have similar fleeting thoughts as they shoot, and they miss a lot more targets than they ought. Trying to shoot in this way makes the whole thing impossible, and even when it works it never feels right. See it, and shoot it.

THE SWING

Swinging the gun means exactly that. It should not be moved in a series of jerks, nor should it be swung and then stopped as the shot is fired. Nor should the gun be swung on its own. The shooter, by turning properly, swings the gun and himself in unison. The gun must never move independently of the shooter because if it does the gun mounting must undergo drastic changes throughout the shot. What starts off as a good gun mount ends with the gun wrapped around the shooters face, or out of his shoulder, or both. At the end of the shot the gun must still be in exactly the same position as it was when it was it first bedded into the face and shoulder, or the relationship between gun, eye and target is destroyed.

TIMING

No matter how good your gun mount, stance, balance and swing, they will all be in vain if you do not pull the trigger at the right moment! With practice the right moment is very apparent, but many shooters ruin an otherwise good shot by hesitating before firing. This is almost always an attempt to improve on the shot, an effort to 'make sure' of hitting the target. This is fatal, because once conscious thought is brought into play those essential instincts, carefully trained through practice, are by-passed.

THE THREE SHOOTING METHODS (figs. 5–6)

Swing through

The swing through method is un- doubtedly the most commonly used of all. It entails swinging the gun from behind the clay, along its flight line, and overtaking it. The shot is fired as the gun begins to pull ahead of the target. It is the only method that can be used for Trap, where the target initially goes away from the gun when it first emerges from the trap house. Arguably this is the most natural of the three methods, and is particularly useful when shooting entirely unknown targets coming from any direction. Nearly all shooting schools teach this method, since it is the method most readily absorbed by beginners and the one employed by almost all game shooters.

Point and swing

This is the method taught by the CPSA, who call it simply 'The Method'. This name suggests that the CPSA considers this to be the only method, and as far as their teaching examinations are concerned this is probably true. Swing through is regarded as old fashioned, while maintained lead is looked down upon. This is unfortunate, since all three methods have merit.

Point and swing is very similar to swing through, except that the gun starts on the target rather than behind it, and then pulls away in front. Arguably it eliminates one of the major errors in shot gun shooting, that of mounting the gun statically before beginning the swing. Point and swing is fine for Sporting but, as with maintained lead, is impossible for Trap, where the gun is inevitably pointing behind the target at the commencement of each shot. Only swing through will work on these disciplines.

a

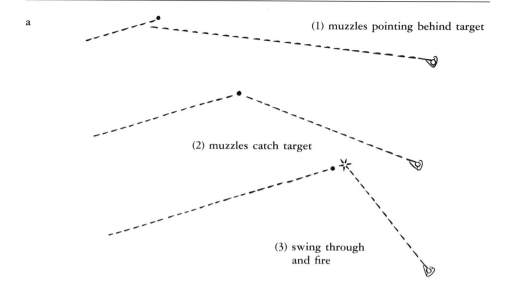

(1) muzzles pointing behind target

(2) muzzles catch target

(3) swing through
and fire

b

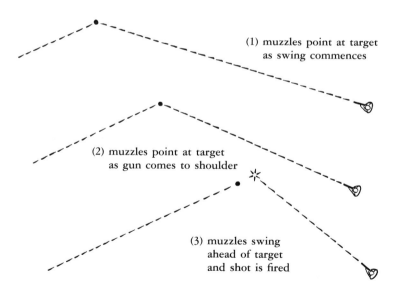

(1) muzzles point at target
as swing commences

(2) muzzles point at target
as gun comes to shoulder

(3) muzzles swing
ahead of target
and shot is fired

Fig. 5 *Shooting methods viewed from above:
(a) swing through, (b) point and swing, (c)
maintained lead*

c

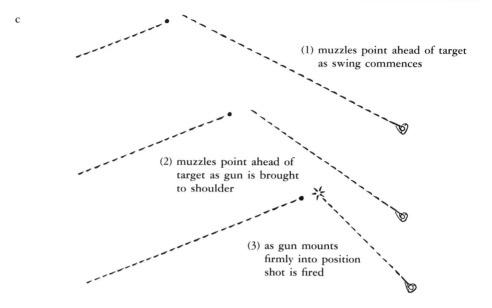

(1) muzzles point ahead of target
as swing commences

(2) muzzles point ahead of
target as gun is brought
to shoulder

(3) as gun mounts
firmly into position
shot is fired

Maintained lead

This is a favourite method among Skeet shooters and an increasing number of Sporting shooters, notably former world champion, John Bidwell. As the name suggests, the gun starts ahead of the target, never behind it or on it, and stays there. When watching a shooter who really has this method under control it looks simplicity itself, and one cannot help but wonder why anyone bothers with the other two methods. Yet maintained lead requires a depth of feel and understanding of shotgun shooting before it can be usefully employed, and is arguably, therefore, not for beginners. It is more easily employed against Skeet targets, which fly on a known fixed line and at a predetermined speed, but less easily on Sporting targets where neither factor is known. Yet John Bidwell teaches this method at his shooting ground in Suffolk, and he has helped many shooters of all standards to achieve good results.

The purpose of any method, of course, is to make it as easy as possible to consistently break the target. Watch top Sporting shooters in action and it can be seen that many of them combine all three methods depending on the type of target. Every shooter must decide on one of the three methods as a general basis for his shooting, but should be well versed in all three in order in order to develop a rounded technique to suit all occasions.

FORWARD ALLOWANCE

Any clay target moving to the left or right, or up or down, will be occupying a different spot in the sky every few milliseconds. It takes several milliseconds for the shot charge to travel even

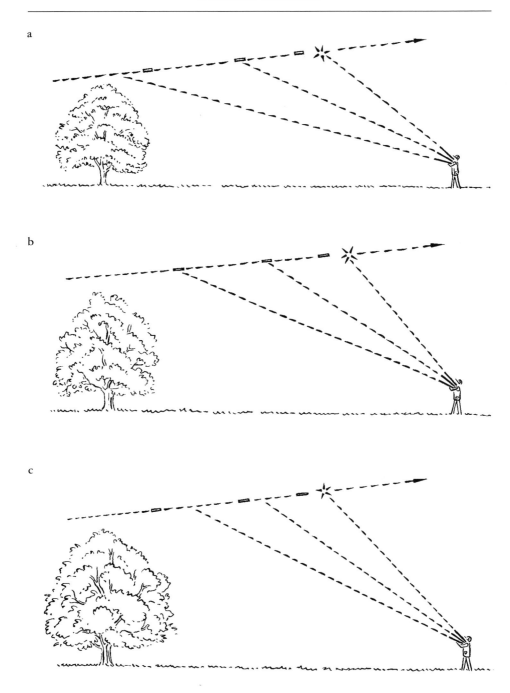

Fig. 6 *Shooting methods viewed from the side:
(a) swing through, (b) point and swing, (c)
maintained lead*

the shortest distance, and many more to travel a distance of 30 yd or over. If you point the gun directly at the target the target will have moved on by the time the shot arrives, and the shot will miss behind. To prevent this happening the shot must be fired ahead of the target, but by how much? This is one of the problems that besets the new shooter, yet a good method can help solve it.

Forward allowance: how much?

One of the most difficult points for one shooter to convey to another is the question of the degree of lead a given target requires. We may know that nearly all targets need some degree of lead, and that a long range and fast crossing target needs more than a close range slow one, but how much more? Two feet? Six feet? Six inches? Who knows? Shotgun shooting is not rifle shooting, where certain hard and fast rules apply. Move the backsight of a rifle one minute of angle on a 100 yd range and the group will move about an inch, regardless of who is using that rifle. Tell three shotgun shooters to lead a target by 6 ft, on the other hand, and you might get three quite different results. Applying the suggestion to lead a target by 6 ft, shooter 'A' might smoke the target. Shooter 'B' might shoot miles ahead of it, while shooter 'C' might contrive to miss behind. Good shotgun shooting depends so much on feel for what the target requires, an ability most shooters refer to as 'reading the target'. How easily you read the target depends

to a large extent on talent, experience and lots of practice. With extensive practice you will shoot many targets without giving any thought to feet and inches. You recognize the target and shoot it accordingly. The more frequently you shoot, and the greater variety of targets you encounter, the more readily you will be able to achieve this.

At the more regulated disciplines, such as Skeet and Trap, the targets fly within certain carefully defined limits. Under these circumstances discovering the feel for each target is a much easier process, since the same targets occur again and again. This is especially true with domestic Skeet and Trap. In the American forms, NSSA Skeet and ATA Trap, it is not unknown for the top performers to run several thousand targets without a miss! At this level concern with lead has been long forgotten, and the winner is the shooter who keeps a cool head and a steady nerve.

Sporting shooters will never realize scores like these, because Sporting course designers are always seeking to produce newer and greater challenges. But even at Sporting there are limits to what a target can be made to do. The more you practise the less likely it is that you will be caught out by targets you simply cannot fathom, and the higher your scores will be.

Of course lead exists, but it is wrong to think in feet and inches: concentrate instead on the feel of each target. That way it will become stored in your subconscious, to arise when the occasion requires it.

14 *Index finger extended down the fore-end, thumb and middle finger of the rear hand linked around the grip. Leading DTL shot, Keith Bond, relaxed but in full control*

5

THE BASICS

I**T IS** an unfortunate fact that in almost all subjects the mastering of the basics is the least interesting part of the learning process. It is unfortunate because, however boring, this process also happens to be the most important. Just as no aspiring mathematician can hope to progress without the ability to add, subtract, multiply and divide, so no shooter can expect to realise his full potential unless he understands and acquires the basic techniques of shooting. Learning a good sound method is vital, but before method must come the basic skills necessary to control the gun.

HOLDING THE GUN

To gain full control of the gun you first must learn how to hold it properly. Hold it too firmly and it will be difficult to move smoothly. Hold it loosely and the gun will leap out of your hands whenever you fire it. Of the two options the latter is far the worst, of course, but neither is ideal. You should hold the gun just firmly enough to maintain control over it at all times, which is no firmer than you would grasp a racquet.

Rear hand

The position of the rear hand is determined by the pistol grip which is a feature of almost all over-and-under guns. There is a right way and several wrong ways to grip the gun at this point. Many beginners will concentrate on what their trigger fingers are doing, and ignore the others. The thumb usually gets least attention, and is often left straight along the top of the grip, so that it sits behind, or worse still against, the top lever. Placed there the thumb can receive a nasty knock, because even mild recoil can drive the top lever back into the thumb and badly bruise it or even split it. At the very least this will mean that shooting for that day is finished!

The proper position for the thumb is curled over and around the grip (14). With the index finger occupied by the trigger the other three fingers should also curl around the grip, touching each other and not separated. The thumb should then rest on the inside of the middle finger. This unity of thumb and finger prevents the gun from moving in the hand and it gives a strong yet effortless grip.

When loading and closing the gun the index finger must be kept away from the trigger to prevent accidental firing. Ideally it will rest along the stock, just above the trigger, or be extended along the trigger guard. Once the gun is loaded and has been raised to the ready position the index finger can then be brought into contact with the trigger.

You can pull the trigger either with the pad of the finger or with the first joint. The pad is the most sensitive part of the finger, but some shooters feel this gives a less precise timing to the shot than when the unyielding first joint is used. Whichever you use make sure that there is a space between the middle finger and the trigger guard, or that finger can get knocked during recoil.

Forward hand

Most clay guns have relatively long fore-ends, allowing plenty of room to find the ideal position for the leading hand. It should be noted that this hand is not intended just as a support for the gun: it must be used as an aid to point the gun to the target. If the hand is positioned too far back, close to the action, then it will not be able to point the gun properly, and the gun will just pivot around it. If the fore-end is held too far forward then the arm becomes overstretched, and the gun will feel long and difficult to mount. The straight left arm, much favoured by generations of game shooters, is out of place for clay shooting. This 'long arm' style evolved in the driven game field, and although it works well in that context for those who employ it, it is too inflexible for clay shooting.

It is important not to allow the hand to get under the fore-end, because this puts strain on the arm. If you extend both hands in front of you, palms facing, it feels very comfortable. Now turn the hands palm upwards and tightness in the elbow joint and forearm is immediately apparent. In a good grip the palm will face the side of the fore-end, not the bottom of it, and the grip will be in the fingers. The thumb should lie along the fore-end, pointing to the target. Some shooters like to extend their index finger and even the middle fingers so that they lie along the fore-end, and providing you can still control the gun and not lose it when the shot is fired, this is a good position. It is one favoured by many Trap shooters (15).

HEAD POSITION

It is often said that the shooter's head should never move, either as the gun is being mounted or once it is in position in the shoulder. This can cause confusion, however. Obviously the head must move, since during a shot the body is in some sort of motion all the time, either turning or bending, or both, and the head must move with it. The fact is, the head must move only to follow what the body is doing. The mistake is to lower the head to the gun as it is being mounted, or worse still to raise the head from the stock just before the shot is fired. Dropping the head to meet the stock is quite common, and even some very good shots do it. The drawback is that the head may drop a different amount for each shot, and will throw out the eye–gun–target relationship so vital to good shooting.

15 *This ABT shooter shows a popular position with his leading hand, but could sacrifice full control of the gun with that loose right hand grip*

You can live with a small head movement of this kind, but what will destroy any prospect of good shooting is the tendency to raise the head from the stock during the shot or just before the shot is fired. Top shooters do this very rarely, yet many poor shooters do it on almost every target. This is a major reason for them being poor shots! Lifting the head off the stock means you completely alter the eye–gun–target relationship. The eye plays the same part as the backsight on a rifle. Provided the eye remains in the same position relative to the gun then your shots will hit the target. Move the eye about, though, and the whole thing is thrown out of kilter: goodbye target.

The positive approach

There are usually quite different mental attitudes behind these head movements. The shooter who drops his head to the stock is being positive and aggressive. Rather like the boxer who lowers his head and comes forward this shooter is making a determined attack on the target. Provided the movement is not overdone he might actually shoot better than if he were to keep his head absolutely still. The head lifter is doing quite the opposite. He fears that he will miss the target, raises his head tentatively to see the target better (so he thinks), and does not confidently commit himself to the shot. When he misses, as he will, his fear of missing grows and so the fault gets worse. The trick is to keep the head firmly on the gun throughout the shot. Concentrating on this one point can often improve a poor shooter's performance amazingly.

THE GUN'S POSITION IN THE SHOULDER

The problem

If your arm is a mass of bruises after every session then the gun is several inches out of its proper position. There are two reasons why this position is undesirable. The immediately obvious one is that it is very painful to fire a gun from the arm. Less obvious is that if the stock strays out of the shoulder and onto the arm then, all other factors being equal, the muzzle will move in the opposite direction and will not point at the target. It is simple enough to prove this. Just mount the gun properly into the shoulder and then shift the stock out onto the arm. The muzzles are immediately off line. The natural correction for this fault is to shift the head across to the stock, hoping to cure one fault with another. Some people manage to shoot accurately with the gun mounted like this, but usually not for long. No one can tolerate being knocked about like this. You might imagine you can endure it, and perhaps you can. But after a certain number of shots (very few if you shoot two days in succession) your concentration will begin to wander from the target. Soon that sharp clout on the arm will totally occupy your thoughts and it is little wonder that you begin to flinch as you pull the trigger. Once you start flinching your shots can go anywhere. Shotgun shooting is not meant to be painful (16)! There are some shooting events where it is not unknown for 1,000 targets to be shot in a single day, and yet if you mount the gun on your arm you won't be able to tolerate even 100.

16 *Halfway into a shot with the gun still coming up to the shoulder. Yet for many struggling shooters this is the fully mounted position – painful and likely to cause a miss!*

Solution A: correct position

Most shooters who suffer with this problem do so because their shoulders are aligned almost to the target. Standing like this there is no way that the gun can sit in the shoulder: it is forced out onto the arm. Assuming you are shooting a target flying straight away, a line through the shoulders should be at 45 degrees to the target. In a correct gun mount the shoulder then hunches forward and up to meet the gun, creating a perfect bed for the stock to sit in.

The position is an inch or so inboard of the point of the arm, between that point and the chest. Even a slightly built shooter will have a pad of muscle there when the shoulder is hunched forward, and this will provide the ideal cushion for the gun to recoil onto.

Solution B: absorbing recoil through the hands and arms

Having described the right place in the shoulder for the gun it would be wrong to think that the shoulder then absorbs all the recoil: it does not. The hands and arms also take their fair share, and with practice it will be found that the hands and arms take much of it. Trick shooters fire the majority of their shots with the gun deliberately out of the shoulder, taking all the recoil with their hands and arms. This does not mean you can let the gun stray out onto your arm, though. Even the modest amount of recoil that reaches the arm will still be sufficient to cause discomfort, and remember too that this sort of mismount can often cause poor aligment with the target.

READY POSITION

The ready position, or pre-mount position, is a factor in all disciplines, even the gun-up Trap disciplines. It is the position which precedes the mounting of the gun to the shoulder, and a given shooter will use the same ready position from shot to shot. The purpose of the ready position is to assist the actual gun mount. Poor shots will often carry the gun in all sorts of odd positions immediately prior to a shot: sometimes with the barrels pointing at the ground, sometimes with them pointing vertically. This inconsistent start position invariably means an inconsistent gun mount, which in turn means missed targets.

Unless the rules state otherwise (as in ISU Skeet) a good start position is as follows: the barrels should point about 20 degrees above the horizontal with the comb of the stock just level with the armpit. Some authorities insist that the stock is drawn back into the armpit, the point of this being that the leading hand is then obliged to push forward to begin the gun mount. Others are not so fussy, and are happy if the stock is lower than the muzzles and resting lightly against the chest at armpit level.

PRACTICE

There really is no excuse for poor gun mounting, since you can learn very good form without having to fire a shot. Practise holding the gun properly, and handle it as much as you can. Learn the elements of good gun mounting and repeat the movement from ready position to shoulder until it is absolutely second nature. A mirror can help here, since you can watch yourself in action and check that the gun is coming into the right position. Eventually this is something you just feel to be right, without any need for mirror assistance. Then the best place to practise is in a darkened room. This prevents distractions and also stops you from becoming too aware of the rib or bead as you practise. This is a minor pitfall, and certainly you must not practise looking anywhere but at the target: hence the darkened room.

While making this practice do not get sloppy with your stance or weight distribution. Always stand properly, feet properly positioned, and as you mount the gun allow your weight to transfer slightly to the forward foot.

17 *Shooting schools are the quickest way of learning to shoot. Instructor Don Wilkinson shows the way*

6

SHOOTING SCHOOLS

A GOOD shooting school provides the highest level of instruction available to the shotgun shooter (17). If the school is busy, and good ones are often booked up for the major part of the season, then the instructors will usually give upwards of a thousand lessons in a year. Granted a good grounding in shooting and teaching methods, the shooting instructor will soon have a wealth of experience on which he can call to sort out just about any shooting problem.

The CPSA coach

When contemplating taking shooting lessons it is important not to confuse the professional instructor with a CPSA coach. The function of a CPSA-trained coach is to offer advice to club shooters who need help at a basic level. Beyond that, while the role of the CPSA coach must not be ignored, he cannot be compared with the instructors at a good shooting school. No matter how long the CPSA coach may have been shooting and coaching at clubs he will not match the experience of a professional instructor. Nor, for that matter, is he

likely to have developed that sixth sense found in the best instructors, that allows them to communicate easily with the cross-section of egos and personalities that make up the world of shooting.

What makes a good instructor?

Understanding what makes someone tick is very important if you hope to improve their shooting. Not everyone receives instruction gladly, even if, as at a shooting school, they are paying quite a lot of money for just that very service. So the good shooting instructor will quickly weigh up his pupil and act accordingly. Some people need to be coaxed gently, some need straight talking, some react to the sergeant major treatment and others respond positively to bullying. Try bullying the man who needs coaxing, though, and the instructor will get nowhere fast and will probably never see that client again!

Although the instructor will adjust his manner to suit his pupil he is likely to be a good deal less flexible about the style he teaches him. Most of the leading schools ensure that the instructors teach the same style, and it is not surprising that they should do so. If an instructor is unavailable a client must be able to go to any of that instructor's colleagues and be taught the same techniques. This tends to mean that a similar degree of swapping is not possible between instructors from different schools, however. For instance Holland & Holland Shooting School and West London Shooting Ground, two of the best known in the UK, are only five miles apart as the crow flies, yet they are very much further apart in the styles and methods they teach.

TWO DIFFERENT SCHOOLS OF SHOOTING

Holland & Holland teach a slightly modified Churchill style, which requires the shooter to stand relatively square to his target. The famous gunmaker and shooting instructor Robert Churchill devised this style, and taught it with great success at his Crayford shooting ground in Kent. He taught that all targets going to the left should be shot with the weight predominantly over a rigid left leg, the right foot pivoting around as in a golf swing. For right targets, Churchill stated, the weight should be over the right leg, the left foot pivoting around. High targets were to be taken with the weight on the rear foot, the body bending backwards, low targets with the weight on the front foot. Churchill's great protegé, the late Norman Clarke, brought a slightly modified Churchill style to Holland & Holland Shooting School, and it is this that is now taught by all Holland's instructors.

West London Shooting Ground teaches the quite different Stanbury style, named after the great shot Percy Stanbury, who worked for many years as West London's chief instructor. His style entails taking all targets, regardless of height and direction, with the weight on the leading foot. The stance is more sideways on than that of the Churchill style, which in turn can affect gun fit. Although the two schools of thought share more similarities than differences it does not do for the shooter to hop between them.

Although not as a matter of policy, West London has spread the Stanbury style far and wide. This is the result of many of its leading instructors setting up their own, usually successful, schools. Among these are Michael Rose, who runs a shooting complex in the Dominican Republic; David Olive, who owns Apsley Shooting School, Peter Crabtree, Steve Denny and Don Wilkinson.

It is interesting to compare the two distinct styles, Stanbury and Churchill, because nearly all the schools in the country teach one or the other. Without doubt, however, the Stanbury style has the greatest following. Let's look at the two styles and their various differences.

The Stanbury style

Stanbury taught a style that is ideal for a man of his build. Stanbury was tall, slim and flexible, and inevitably the style he developed made good use of his physical characteristics. His front foot would be almost directly in front of his rear, so that the two were nearly on a line to his front. With his body at about 45 degrees to the front, Stanbury could turn easily through 90 degrees left or right, his weight always over a straight leading leg, the rear foot, heel raised, just providing sufficient contact with the ground to maintain balance. Leaning forward allowed him to take the lowest of driven targets, while arching back, still with his weight on that forward leg, allowed him to handle high overhead targets, even those that perhaps had gone beyond the vertical. Stanbury's shooting technique was later adopted by the CPSA as its standard coaching method, called by them 'The Method', as though there were no other! The method works like this. The shooter focusses his attention on the target. The muzzles are placed on the target prior to mounting the gun. The muzzles then move with the target as the gun is being mounted. The gun accelerates ahead of the target as the gun comes to the shoulder and the shot is fired, the classic moving gun mount. An awareness of lead is basic to this method, although this must not suggest any conscious aiming in the rifle sense of the word.

The Churchill method

To be entirely accurate this should be renamed the Norman Clarke method, since few people now teach Churchill in its 'pure' fashion. Churchill's unmodified method, as recommended in his books, was devised partly to promote the sale of his 25 in barrel guns. It involved pointing the muzzles at the target, Stanbury style, then making a very fast moving gun mount which culminated in the shot being fired right at the target. The theory was that the required forward allowance would be achieved automatically, this by the fast moving gun, aided by short barrels, coupled with the delay between the intention to fire and the actual pulling of the trigger: the shooting man's nirvana! Sadly it is literally a very hit and miss method, and few people use it with any degree of success. Despite this there are those who still advocate this method in print, although it must be said they are not renowned for their own shooting ability!

Norman Clarke used the Churchill footwork but discarded his old mentor's 'swipe and fire' technique. Instead he would have his pupil swing the gun from behind the target and then through it and fire. The end result was exactly that achieved by Stanbury's method: a moving gun that tracked away from the target as the shot was fired. Clarke believed that starting the swing behind the target encouraged the shooter to swing through the target. There is actually no right or wrong in either method, since both have produced fine shots.

The good clay shooter will adapt these methods to suit his needs, and often his technique will include elements of both, depending on the target. Maintained lead will be in there, too, although with few exceptions this is a method most schools choose to avoid.

THE FUNCTION OF THE SHOOTING SCHOOL

As a short cut to good shooting the shooting school takes some beating. Learning to shoot can sometimes be a miserable process if unguided, not the least because there are so many false trails down which to wander. As with most physical activities, you will absorb poor technique just as readily as good, and once bad habits are acquired they are difficult to eradicate. This is the other function of the school: analysing and curing problems. Trying alone to sort out a persistent problem can be a soul destroying exercise. The reason for this is that you cannot see yourself shoot, and any ideas you might have had about the problems and its cure tend to be subjective. Even if you happen to hit on the right answers you cannot stand back and see that you are putting the cure into effect. This is where good instruction is invaluable.

Shooting schools can only be judged on their respective merits, and over the years they have proven themselves time and again. The one apparent drawback with the school is the cost of the lessons, which might put their services beyond the pockets of many shooters. Yet how do you assess cost and value? The shooting school provides a good service, at a price, and brings the shooter to a relatively high performance standard in a short time. The initial outlay might be high, but how do you evaluate this when comparing it to perhaps years of little or no progress when you try to work the whole thing out for yourself?

SKEET AND TRAP

Unfortunately, whereas instruction in general shotgun shooting is widely available, this instruction is aimed predominently at the game and Sporting shooter. The Skeet or Trap shooter with a problem to iron out has less choice. There are a number of coaches skilled in DTL or English Skeet instruction, but very few in the international games. In recent years coaching in these disciplines has become available through the efforts of the British International Board, the body responsible for the organisation of international shooting in the UK. Coaching schemes are now in place, with the likes of international shooters Peter Croft and Joe Neville offering their services. With the growing interest in international shooting it is to be hoped that these schemes will expand to include newcomers to the sport as well as those already involved. The UK has produced some excellent international shooters over the years: how much better might standards be with dedicated coaching?

PART THREE

Competitive Shooting

7

SPORTING SHOOTING

SPORTING: A BRIEF HISTORY

SPORTING IS without doubt the most popular clay shooting game in the UK, and it is rapidly becoming equally popular around the world. Yet it has taken an incredibly long time to catch on outside of the UK. The reason for this slow acceptance elsewhere is difficult to understand, since a basic Sporting shoot requires little investment beyond a few manual traps and a field or wood to throw the targets. How different from Skeet or Trap! A Skeet field needs two purpose-built houses, two electrically linked traps, preferably automatic, and a specially laid out shooting area. Down the Line, the most basic Trap discipline, is somewhat less expensive to install than a Skeet field; but an Olympic Trap layout, using fifteen automatic machines, an acoustic release system and a computer, costs as much as a very decent up-market saloon car.

It was shooting schools that opened the way for Sporting shooting in the UK. These schools provided, and still provide, the means by which the game

shot could practise his game shooting technique. Clays thrown from towers, over ponds, across fields and over hedges provided an interesting and varied array of targets comparable with the real thing, and shooters soon found that they enjoyed shooting these targets for their own sake. As shooters became more proficient so the targets were made increasingly more difficult, and once a set of rules and regulations were formulated Sporting rapidly became a popular discipline. There are three types of Sporting shooting:

- English Sporting – the rules for which are formulated by the English CPSA.
- FITASC Sporting – the ultimate Sporting discipline, featuring as it does a far greater variety of targets than those of English Sporting (18).
- Supersporting – a relatively new Sporting game, this is an interesting development which

18 *FITASC Sporting is the ultimate Sporting clays challenge*

Arrival of the O/U

The British Open Sporting Championships, still the most important English Sporting event in the world, has seen the emergence of many fine shooters. Percy Stanbury and Joe Wheater were legendary figures of the early Sporting scene, with Wheater recognised as possibly the finest all-round shot of all time. In Stanbury's time the side-by-side gun dominated, largely because the over-and-under was little known in the UK. The O/U was treated with suspicion by the traditionalists, who saw it as a 'foreign' weapon. This was despite the fact that very fine O/Us were produced by the great English gunmakers, although the high prices of these weapons eliminated from ownership all but the very wealthiest of shooters. Wheater did great shooting with a side-by-side but shot better still when he changed to an O/U. He had felt, rightly, that foreign shooters with their O/Us had an advantage, and once he had changed to this style of gun, in the Fifties, he never went back to the side-by-side. It was inevitable that the rest of the UK soon adopted the O/U, setting aside their firearm xenophobia in favour of improved shooting. Nowadays no one who shoots clays with serious intent uses a side-by-side.

employs certain aspects of both English and FITASC Sporting.

Sadly for the many who love to shoot it, while being more varied than English Sporting, FITASC Sporting is expensive in every respect, and its high price is one of the reasons why it will never replace the English version.

Supersporting was originally devised by the famous British gun company, Gunmark, and though more varied than English Sporting is less so than FITASC. It uses three traps per stand, allowing several double permutations, a–c, a–b, b–c, as well as simultaneous, following and report pairs. This avoids the repetition of ordinary English Sporting targets, yet it remains relatively inexpensive. In 1991 the British Sporting championship was shot for the first time using the Supersporting format, and it provided the most testing course ever for that event.

Since the Fifties O/Us and clay shooting have grown enormously in popularity. When the British Sporting championship was first held, back in 1927, it was a one day event with a relatively small entry. The modern championship occupies five days, soon to be expanded to six, with an entry of over 1,500 shooters (19).

In the USA, the country with probably the largest leisure shooting community in the world, Trap and Skeet have dominated the clay scene for many years. Some clubs dabbled with Sporting, but lighthearted Sporting clay games such as 'Crazy Quail' underlined the Americans' lack of serious intest in Sporting as a discipline. It was not until

the Eighties that Sporting began to make inroads in the USA, largely due to the efforts of people like Chris Cradock, an elder statesman of the UK clay scene. He and others showed the Americans what Sporting was all about, and after several half hearted beginnings the game suddenly took off in the USA in a very big way. Sporting clays, US style, is now beginning to catch up with Trap and Skeet, and following the Americans' keen involvement Sporting

is gaining a foothold in many other countries, too.

The International Shooting Union, the body that governs all shooting disciplines featured in the Olympics, recognizes two clay disciplines, Olympic Skeet and Olympic Trap, with ISU Double Trap a recent third. To date there is no Sporting discipline in the Olympics, but with the growing world interest in the game it is surely inevitable that this situation will soon be

19 *The British Open Sporting Championship attracts over 1,500 shooters each year*

corrected. Since the ISU likes its Olympic disciplines to be contained within a relatively small area, essential if spectators and television are to take an interest, it is likely that Olympic Sporting will have to be a far more compact game than it is at present. It is highly likely that any ISU Sporting discipline will employ existing facilities for Skeet and Trap, with probably an additional trap or traps positioned on or around the Skeet and Trap field to add extra interest.

THE SPORTING SCENE

It is no surprise to learn that the UK has a tremendous depth of Sporting talent. On any weekend in country areas a shooter need not travel far to find a good 30, 40 or 50 target shoot with cash and trophy prizes on offer, and during the warmer months there will be plenty of larger events too, often with big prizes. Many of the UK's leading performers have cut their teeth shooting perhaps six or more of the smaller shoots in a weekend, scooping up the prizes as they go. But winning is not as easy as it once was, even at these minor events. Every area has its local hotshots who on these smaller shoots can offer the leading lights a good run for their money. Most of these locals seldom stray from their home areas, and few bother to obtain CPSA classification. When they do they often effortlessly slip immediately into 'AA' class, to add their names to the long list of first class UK registered Sporting shooters.

In international Sporting competition the UK has an enviable record. Despite an ever increasing international entry to these events UK shooters take most, sometimes all, of the gold medals in team and individual classes, although this looks set to change in the future. France and Belgium have some tremendous Sporting shots who have won world and European championships, but neither country has the depth of talent of the UK. Italy, for so long totally absorbed by Skeet and Trap, shows signs of taking an interest in Sporting, and if they were to make a serious effort they would represent a very strong force on the European scene. The greatest challenge will surely come from the USA, a country with huge numbers of excellent Trap and Skeet shooters, many of whom are changing their allegiance and turning to the new challenge of Sporting. World and Olympic ISU, Skeet champion, Matt Dryke, is already making his mark on the US Sporting scene, as is ISU Skeet and Trap champion, Dan Carlisle. Both these men, along with US shooters like Jon Kruger, seem destined to carry off international Sporting honours before many more seasons have elapsed. In the meantime the USA has to stand by while leading UK performers like A.J. Smith and John Bidwell pinch the top prizes in the US State championships. How long before this situation is reversed remains to be seen!

SPORTING TARGETS

Defining a Sporting target is not difficult: any clay that flies or rolls along the ground within 50 yd or less of the shooter can be so described. The targets themselves have changed from those originally presented, however. No longer is the familiar black 110 mm standard target the only clay shown. There are:

• Fast 90 mm midis
• Tiny 60 mm minis
• Lumbering and misnamed rockets
• Rolling and bouncing rabbits
• Ducking and weaving wafer-thin battues

Colours range from bright orange to yellow, white, green and even pink, while some clays explode in a spectacular burst of brightly-coloured powder when hit. Each of the targets mentioned has flight characteristics all its own, and each presents the shooter with a slightly different problem:

Standard

The 108–110 mm standard is the most popular target, and it is likely that at least 75 per cent of all Sporting targets thrown are standards. This target flies very steadily, and although it is decelerating from the moment it leaves the trap this is not noticable except at the very end of its flight, when the standard will glide gently to the ground. The standard is usually shot within 50 yd of its leaving the trap, when it still has a good head of steam. A half decent hit on this target will ensure a break, even at longer ranges.

Midi

Many shooters consider this little 90 mm disc to be the ideal Sporting target. It has sufficient mass to maintain good speed over a long distance, and being lighter than the standard target

the midi comes off the trap arm a good deal faster. A fairly feeble trap that struggles with standard targets will often be transformed when set to throw midis.

At medium and long ranges it is very easy to confuse the midi with the standard target, and where there is any doubt the shooter should always ask the referee exactly what it is he is shooting at. Shooting at a 40 yd standard, which turns out to be a 30 yd midi, will lead to some frustrating misses! A super little target, it breaks quite easily even with small shot.

Mini

The mini is something of a novelty target, being too small and light to maintain speed beyond 30 yd or so. Beyond this range the mini slows right down and only floats gently forwards, even in still air. Against a head wind the mini will often turn round and float back to where it has come from, a manoeuvre guaranteed to cause confusion in the ranks! It only needs a flick from a single pellet to break the mini, although mentioning this fact to a shooter who has just missed a bucketful of the little horrors might produce some colourful language. A good Skeet cartridge will handle this target at all but the longest ranges, and even then 8s will do a good job.

Battue

The thin battue comes off the trap arm very fast, and maintains this speed until it eventually rolls over and accelerates into the ground. It can be thrown either way up, and if it is placed upside down in the trap it will roll over and dive very soon after leaving the trap arm, a characteristic favoured by many shooting grounds. Shooters encountering the battue for the first time are often baffled by its speed and its twisting flight, particularly when it has to be shot as a crosser. Under these circumstances the battue presents its very thin edge, almost invisible, and most shooters wait for the inevitable roll over before shooting. At this point the target shows its whole face, and even a flick from a single pellet will knock off a piece and score as a hit. Half a second after the battue has rolled, though, it becomes an elusive target indeed, looping downwards and accelerating. Sometimes, sadistic shoot organisers will present the battue in such a way that it only rolls when it is a long way down range, beyond the reach of any shotgun pattern. In these circumstances the battue must be shot edgeways on, and it really takes some seeing. Once it is hit, though, the edgeways on battue still breaks quite easily. Seeing it then hitting it is the tricky part!

Rocket

Some clay manufacturers prefer to call this target 'special battue', perhaps concerned that calling it a rocket could lead to prosecution under the Trades Description Act! The rocket is similar in build to a rabbit target, and being both thick and dense it comes relatively slowly off the trap arm. Once on its way it just keeps going at a steady plod. Although it is the same diameter its extra density makes it harder to break than a standard target, and beyond 25 yd a crossing rocket is not a target to

tackle with small shot and Skeet chokes. Some of the recently introduced automatic teal traps work best with these targets, and since this usually means that the target is showing its vulnerable face to the shooter it is not too difficult to break. Edgeways on, though, it needs a good pattern to break it. A decent Trap cartridge, with 7 or $7\frac{1}{2}$ shot, is a must.

Rabbit

There are two types of rabbit target: the manual rabbit and the auto rabbit. The manual rabbit, made for manually operated traps, is quite robust but is not difficult to break if it is hit squarely. The auto rabbit target is another proposition entirely, though. This is a much beefier target, one that seems capable of absorbing a lot of punishment without breaking. Unfortunately, although an automatic rabbit trap will not accept manual rabbits it is quite easy to throw the auto rabbit target from a manual trap. To be sure of a break ignore the more open chokes when dealing with rabbits, unless they are very close (less than 20 yd), and keep your Skeet ammunition in the bag.

SHOOTING STANDS

In the early days of Sporting the various shooting stands were named according to the type of live bird they represented. Nowadays, although many Sporting shoots retain this idea of naming stands, many others simply number stands and ignore any sort of type description. The reason is that few stands truly represent any particular type of bird, especially in major events. This is because Sporting targets have become progressively more testing as shooting standards have risen, and it is certain that the average game shooter would not venture a shot at many Sporting targets, were they live birds. Without doubt, a shooter who competed at Sporting clays in the Thirties would have quite a shock were he to take part in a modern Sporting shoot.

HANDLING SPORTING TARGETS

Such is the tremendous variety of targets thrown throughout the year at all the many Sporting clay shoots in the world, that to try mention all of them, and all the possible combinations, would need a book many times larger than this one. Most Sporting targets, though, fall into one of several categories, since targets can only fly or roll up, down, left or right. However, there is a lot of difference to the type of approach necessary to handle a low and close quartering target, flying away, to that required for a high crossing target that happens to be diving. The following is a look at some of some of the targets typically encountered at a Sporting shoot, and how the best shooters handle them.

SPRINGING TEAL

The Springing Teal target is a certain feature of any good Sporting layout, and it may appear as a single target when it is part of a combination double, or as a simultaneous double. By definition, all springing teal targets zoom skywards on a near vertical trajectory, and they can be anything from quite simple to very difficult. The easier teal are those

which go up and away from the shooter, showing their full diameter as they rise. The shooter has only the one plane to worry about. If that same target is thrown up and to the left or right then this brings an extra dimension to the shot, since the target is now moving to the side as well as rising.

Shooting the straight teal (20)
Provided the rules of the shoot allow, there are three places this target can be shot:

- On the way up
- As it peaks and briefly stops
- As it falls

Of the three the first is to be preferred. The shooter is positively attacking the target, and will time the shot better. In the second option something akin to a rifle type shot is employed, bordering on a deliberate aim. The target is allowed to climb to its peak and then stop, and the shot is fired right at it. The third option should only be used when there is no alternative. This often occurs when two teal targets are thrown from the same trap. By the time the first has been shot the second has peaked and is beginning to fall back.

Shooting on the way up
Half the battle with Springing Teal is knowing where to point the gun prior to calling for the target. The ideal spot is halfway up the target's flight path. Point the gun lower than this and it is very difficult to catch the target. Point it higher and the shot is in danger of becoming a poke with a stationary gun.

Most teal targets jump up fast, and if you point the gun around about half-way then you have time to see the target clearly before you move. Ideally, the gun will start to move just as the target passes the muzzle, then it is a simple matter to keep the the target focussed, swing the gun up the target's flight path as you mount the gun and shoot just after the muzzles overtake it. This target needs just as much follow through as any crossing target, and most misses occur because the shooter stops the gun just as he fires.

Shooting at the peak

Some shooters love to take this target right at the peak of its flight. This works well enough except when the targets are flying out as well as up, as happens when there is a tail wind, or when they start 30 yd or more in front of the shooter. The peaking teal target may then present a shot of some 40 yd or more, and if there is anything of a breeze the target will not come to a convenient stop, but will wander with the wind. This makes it a very tricky proposition! If the second target of a double is slowing up dramatically just as you catch it, however, then don't hesitate: shoot right at it with an almost stationary gun.

Shooting the falling teal

This should only be attempted when there is no alternative. The problem with the dropping teal is that it is gradually accelerating towards the ground. The further you allow it to drop the

faster it becomes, and handling this calls for an accelerating down-swing of the gun. Keeping the muzzles on line is half the trick, because the dropping target will sometimes curl in any breeze that might be present. Keep your eyes hard on the target, and get the gun moving well underneath it. Make sure the muzzles are still moving downwards after the shot is fired. Some shooters always take their teal targets in this fashion, yet very few of the top shooters will attempt it unless forced by circumstances: enough said.

RABBITS

Why is that what ought to be one of the easier targets encountered in a Sporting event is often the one that causes the most trouble? Spectate at any Sporting stand where rabbits are a feature and you will see much head shaking and plenty of misses. Many shooters fear the rabbit target, yet it is one of the slowest and it is never affected by wind. There are several reasons for its unpopularity.

Bounce

The rabbit's one deviation from a true roll happens when the rabbit target hits a bump. It springs into the air, sometimes flying for several yards. The average shooter dreads this happening, yet the top shooters love it! Once the rabbit has left the ground it really is a doddle. It won't deviate from its course, it is slow, and with a decent swing this airborne rabbit will be killed every time.

Handling the rabbit target

The first important point to remember

20 *Most Sporting shoots will feature a teal stand*

Misreading misses

Listen when a group of friends are struggling to hit a rabbit target. Fred shoots and misses. Everyone, including Fred, agrees he is behind. Fred then gives the rabbit an extra foot or two lead. Again he misses, still his friends cry: 'Behind!' Certainly, the dust kicked up by the pellets striking the ground suggest that Fred is behind. More likely than not, Fred was in front from the first, yet he and his friends were fooled by that dust. This can also cause people to think they are hitting the rabbit target yet it won't break. Fred says: 'That rabbit was right in the centre of my pattern!' There are dark mumblings about 'concrete' targets, and Fred carries on missing. What is happening is something of an optical illusion. The shot is fired too far ahead of the rabbit, yet at the instant the pellets strike the ground there is no dust at all. A fraction of a second later the dust starts to rise, but by this time the rabbit has moved a good two feet further forward. Another fraction of a second passes and the dust rises in clouds, yet the clouds are now behind the rabbit, creating the illusion that the shot has also gone behind. When the shot has missed even further in front, the rabbit is surrounded by dust, giving the impression that it is bullet proof: hence the cries of 'Hard targets!'

is that rabbits are not that quick. Often, in order to make them more of a challenge, the shoot organiser will specify that the rabbit has to be hit between two marks, often a pair of straw bales 20 or so yards apart. A flying target would be a much trickier proposition in such a confined space (21).

The rabbit target lends itself very well to the maintained lead method of shooting. The muzzles are positioned well out from the place where the rabbit first appears, and as soon as the target is seen the gun is set in motion, with the muzzles pointing ahead of the target. The moving gun is brought smoothly to the mounted position and is fired without hesitation as it beds into the shoulder. It is essential to follow through.

The swing through method is more difficult to employ, especially when the rabbit is only visible for a short period. The gun has to be swung very quickly in order to catch and pass the target, and the whole thing looks and feels something of a thrash. Maintained lead allows a much smoother and slower swing, which gives that much more control.

TOWER TARGETS

Targets launched from towers provide some of the most entertaining shots encountered on a Sporting shoot. Towers come in all shapes and sizes. Some, like the white skyscraper at Roundwood Shooting Ground, throw targets that are right on the edge of shotgun range. Towers like this frequently ruin an otherwise good scorecard. Others, just a few yards in height, can still produce good testing targets.

Why so difficult?

A tower target is often difficult for two reasons. One is sheer range: a target from a high tower, particularly a crosser, can be right on the limit of a shotgun's ability to achieve a good break. The degree of forward allowance required for a truly long shot, one of 40 yds or more, is not proportional to that necessary for closer targets. For instance, if a 20 yd crossing target needs 3 ft of lead it does not follow that one at 40 yd at a similar angle requires 6 ft. This is because the shot charge quickly loses velocity, and it is likely that our 40 yd crossing target needs 10 ft lead or more if the target is to be centred. The sight picture on such

a target is unique, and it needs plenty of experience and practice to acquire it. Once you understand the sight picture a good swing is vital to success.

The key to success

On a dead straight high bird there are two methods commonly employed to make a successful shot. One is to bend backwards so that the gun travels in a straight line through and ahead of the target (22). Many shooters manage to swing the gun through and ahead of the target, but then they allow the swing to slow, and even stop, as they fire. The shot inevitably goes well behind. With this type of swing-slow-stop action the

21 In theory the easiest of Sporting targets, the Rabbit stand can often be the downfall of even the best shooters!

apparent forward allowance can be doubled, and still the target will be missed behind. The critical part of a good swing occurs after the gun has overtaken the target. By continuing the bend backwards the shooter must accelerate the gun away in front of the target as he pulls the trigger. He must not look at the space ahead of the target as he does so: he must keep the target firmly in focus throughout the shot. It is this swinging-through-and-away action that breaks the target, not swinging out ahead and stopping.

The other method on high straight targets is to turn sideways to the target and treat it like a crosser. This is a good method for the man who must shoot with an eye closed. For him, using the bending backwards method the target means the target is obscured by his barrels as he overtakes it. By turning sideways, though, he can keep his target in view throughout the shot. It must be said, however, that turning sideways in this fashion probably creates as many difficulties as it solves, and few leading shooters resort to this method except in desperate moments when nothing else seems to work!

The crossing high target

For most shooters the crossing high target is the most difficult of all. Seeing the correct sight picture is problem enough but so too is making the proper physical movement required. Many shooters get the sight picture right yet still miss the target: frustrating! The

22 *Sporting champion, Stuart Clark, halfway into a fast and high overhead target*

usual result is that the shooter alters his sight picture and obviously still fails to connect. What is happening? When the sight picture appears perfect and yet the target is missed there must be an elevation problem. Almost certainly the shooter is allowing his shoulders to roll instead of turning them squarely to the target. Rolling the shoulders is a natural but wrong action, and one that on a high target is guaranteed to drag the muzzles down beneath the target flight line. Elevation problems caused by this shoulder rolling are the most difficult for the shooter to detect, yet they would be picked up immediately by an experienced coach or a knowledgeable shooter.

The rolling action described means that on a left crossing target the left shoulder drops, and *vice versa*. A good cure is to practise on these targets while

23 Not all high targets come from towers! Mountainous countryside provides the perfect backdrop for this FITASC championship

concentrating on dropping the opposite shoulder. On a right crosser, for instance, consciously drop the left shoulder. The immediate effect of this is that the muzzles are encouraged to swing up and along the target flight line. Do this and one of the most common causes of missing on high crossers (and *all* crossers, for that matter) is eliminated.

Tower targets from behind

One other tower target that can cause endless problems is the one that appears from behind the shooter and flies away from him, well up in the sky. Forget swing through on this shot: if you start with the muzzles behind this beauty you will probably never catch it! The gun must, of course, be swung on a downward path, and this is very unnatural. The simplest way to handle this one is to get the muzzles moving ahead of the target as soon as it emerges, adjust the sight picture during the gun mount and fire as the gun beds into the shoulder. Classic Move-Mount-Shoot, John Bidwell style!

GOING AWAY TARGETS

The target that flies straight away from the shooter, having been launched besides or directly in front of the shooting stand, is theoretically the simplest of the lot. Yet many otherwise competent Sporting shots make hard work of it (24). One of the reasons for this is that the target is unique in that it needs no swing at all. It's a simple point-and-fire shot. Probably the major problem is a psychological one, however. The target, particularly if it is launched from a fast trap, can give the impression that a snap shot is the only answer to a target apparently flying quickly out of shotgun range. The most common fault occurs when the shooter raises the stock sharply to his shoulder. The gun is into position quickly but this type of gun mount causes the muzzles to dip below the target. If the shot is fired immediately then obviously the target will be missed underneath. If, on the other hand, the shooter delays the shot and raises the muzzles up to the target there is a good chance he will swing over the top of it and miss high.

There is always plenty of time to take this shot, and what is wanted is a very precise gun mount, where the muzzles are held dead on the target as the gun is brought smoothly to the shoulder. Before calling for the target the muzzles should be positioned on the expected flight line of the target. As the target appears the eyes are focussed on it (never on the gun!). The leading hand points the muzzles straight at the target and at the same time the stock is brought smoothly to the shoulder. As the stock beds into the shoulder the shot is fired

24 *The high target from behind is one of the trickier propositions on any Sporting layout. Andy Harvison shows his ready position*

without any hesitation. Any attempt to check alignment by squinting down the rib will almost certainly guarantee a miss.

QUARTERING AWAY TARGETS

This type of shot will feature on many Sporting stands, and it is important not to confuse it with the straightforward going away target (25). However shallow the angle, this target will require a swing, and cannot be tackled successfully by pointing straight at the target with a stationary gun. The important point to make, however, is that quartering targets require nothing like the long swing necessary on full crossing targets. Because the deflection of the target relative to the shooter is quite small it is a mistake to point the gun at or near the trap prior to calling for the target. The muzzles should be positioned well out from the trap (see illustration).

The shooter then has plenty of time to see the target and can allow it to catch and pass the muzzles before starting his shot. With the eye focussed on the target the gun can then be swung up to and through the target and the shot fired just as the gun passes it. Regardless of the speed of the target this shot requires far less lead than a full crossing shot. There are probably as many quartering targets missed ahead as there are those missed behind.

DOUBLES

You can practise until you are brilliant on every kind of single target ever thrown, yet to be good at Sporting you must learn how to handle doubles. Almost every English Sporting stand you encounter will involve the shooting of

25 *A skeet layout utilised for a FITASC competition. Steve Whitelock takes a left to right quartering target from the low house*

81

doubles in one form or another. There are several types of double commonly encountered. Very often targets will be thrown at the same time and from the same trap. To make this double slightly trickier the targets might be different, such as a midi thrown with a standard, or a black with an orange. The following pair is another same-trap double, where the first target is followed by the second as fast as the trapper can load the machine and release it. Some traps are equipped with two separate throwing arms, and these can throw following pairs where the first target is followed by a second, sometimes quite different, target, flying on a different trajectory. The pair on report often feature two different trap positions, the second target being launched only when the first has been fired at. The possible double combinations are endless, too, and while a high tower target combined with a rabbit might be an unusual double it does happen!

There is one golden rule to bear in mind whenever doubles are being shot: there is no such thing as a double! Even if it were possible you never fire both barrels simultaneously, you fire them one at a time, at one target at a time. This is the secret: a double is treated like two single targets. You focus on one target, swing the gun at that one target and shoot it. Having fired at it you then, and only then, transfer your full attention to the second target. This is particularly difficult to achieve on simultaneous doubles, especially when they are flying close together. It is all too easy to look at both at the same time, the focus of attention being some

vague spot between the two. If they are very close together you will occasionally get lucky and hit them both with one shot. More likely, though, you will miss both. Shoot one at a time.

Simultaneous doubles

Let us look first at the most common type of simultaneous double, the one that is thrown from the same trap (26). Observation prior to going on the stand plays an important part here. Although they leave the trap together one target will inevitably fly on a different flight line to the other. One will always be slightly higher or lower, and one will always lead the other. Take the rearmost target first and it will be comparatively easy, having shot this one, to continue the swing onto the second target. Take the leading target first, however, and the gun must then be stopped and brought back to find the second target, an extra movement that takes more time and effort. Where one target is higher than the other always take the lower target first. It is then easy to find the second target over the barrels and make the shot. Shoot the higher target first, on the other hand, and you will have to drop the gun in order to locate that second target. Always make it as easy for yourself as possible.

On simultaneous targets from two traps you must make the decision before going onto the stand as to which of the two you intend taking first. The decision may well be made for you if there

26 *A left to right pair of quartering targets: which to take first?*

27 *A following pair is one of the easiest doubles – provided you can hit the first!*

are several people shooting the stand before you. It is soon apparent which is the right (or wrong) order in which to take them. If this is not possible, however, you will have to make the decision for yourself. It is usually not too difficult to decide. If, for instance, one target drifts easily across your front while the other one tears off into the distance you will obviously opt to take the speedy target first. Having made the choice stick with it, shoot that first target and then go for the second: one at a time.

Following doubles

One target thrown a second after an identical preceding target is usually one of the easier pairs (27). If you can hit one you can hit both. The trick here is to concentrate on taking the first target with full attention focussed on it and it alone. Do not concern yourself with the second. Get the first one shot and then immediately drop the gun slightly from the shoulder and bring the muzzles back to find the second target. Having found it just repeat the mount and swing that successfully shot the first target. The temptation is to rush the first shot, but this is counterproductive. Do not dawdle over it, of course, but give your-

self the chance to make a good swing at the first target. There will be plenty of time for the second.

Doubles on report

This double will invariably mean there are two quite different targets to contend with. The extra difficulty value this entails is eased slightly by the fact that the second target will not appear until you have shot at the first. Each target can be shot just like the single it is, without concern caused by another target in the sky at the same time. Another fact to bear in mind is when the first target is very much easier than the second. Should you miss the first, and

it still presents a reasonable shot, it might make sense to take another shot at this one rather than trying to tackle the harder second target!

THE CASE FOR MAINTAINED LEAD

John Bidwell

One of the finest ambassadors for Sporting shooting in the UK is former FITASC Sporting world champion, John Bidwell. John is one of the few UK clay shooters who has truly capitalized on his success. Besides owning one of the best professional Sporting layouts in the country, High Lodge Shooting Ground near Lowestoft, Suffolk, he also manufactures automatic traps and shooting accessories, gives international shooting clinics and has put together a very enjoyable trick shooting show, too. Most relevant to us, though, is his shooting method, maintained lead, which he has outlined in his best selling book *Move, Mount, Shoot*, written in conjunction with shooting journalist Robin Scott.

Maintained lead vs other methods

Maintained lead is by no means a new method of shooting, having been used for many years by most of the world's leading Skeet shooters, although probably less so in the UK. Of course, long before Skeet was ever thought of, it is certain that with the flint ignition of the early muzzle loaders maintained lead was the only possible method. With modern guns the shot charge is on its way practically the moment the trigger is pulled, any delay being well beyond the ability of humans to detect. With

28 *John Bidwell putting his move-mount-shoot method into action*

29 *Paul Bentley shooting Sporting*

flintlocks, however, there is a definite time lag between the pulling of the trigger and the ignition of the charge. First, when the trigger is pulled, the cock (now known as the hammer) carrying the flint flies forward under spring pressure. In turn the flint scrapes rapidly down the steel, causing a considerable shower of hot metal sparks. The steel simultaneously kicks back, revealing the fine priming powder in the pan. If everything goes to plan (not guaranteed!) the priming powder then ignites, sending a flame through to the main charge: bang. No shooting method dependent on split second ignition could work with a system like this. The flint

shooter must first establish his lead and then pull the trigger. He then maintains this lead until the gun eventually decides to go off. So maintained lead, now seen as the new way to shoot clays, is actually the very oldest of methods. There is nothing new under the sun!

Many Sporting shooters, too, employ maintained lead when the target favours its use, mostly on close crossing targets. Bidwell, though, uses it on all his targets, near and far, which certainly until recently made him unique in this respect.

Swing through and point and swing have long been the two methods favoured for Sporting shooting, the latter simply being a slightly modified version of the former, despite what the CPSA might say. Because both methods work very well on Sporting targets the interaction of a third method might seem unnecessary, even questionable. If maintained lead is only as good as, and no better, than the first two methods, why bother with it? Many shooting instructors, brought up with the idea that swing through is the only method, would say the following when rejecting maintained lead as a possible alternative:

- By starting with the gun on or behind the target the shooter is able subconsciously to judge the speed of the target as he catches it. You cannot do this with maintained lead.
- By the same token the shooter can get the muzzles on the flight line of the target as he is catching it, thus correctly judging the target's line and elevation. You cannot do this with maintained lead.
- By swinging the gun through and away from the target a certain amount of automatic lead is built in, because there is a delay between the intention to fire and the actual pulling of the trigger. With maintained lead this doesn't happen since the gun does not pull away from target.

Of course, the answer to all these criticisms is John Bidwell himself: if he were a struggling 'B' class shooter then his claims could, with justification, be rejected out of hand. When a world champion speaks, however, you ought to pay attention and listen carefully to what he has to say! To the first two points Bidwell says: 'Wrong! You can do all these things using maintained lead', and to the last: 'Right! But with maintained lead you don't have to pull ahead of the target: you are already out in front of it!'

The advantages of maintained lead
So if the claims of established shooting instructors can be met and countered, what does John Bidwell see as the advantages of his method? First is the element of speed. Because he starts behind his target and catches it the 'swing through' practitioner must swing that much faster than the 'maintain leader', who starting in front of his target need only swing in time with the target, not faster. By swinging at its pace he is able to swing slower. Thus with less effort the maintain lead shooter can shoot his targets in the same place in the sky as the swing through man. On the other hand, using the same degree of effort as the swing through man he can shoot a given target quicker. Anyone who has watched Bidwell shooting cannot but be impressed by the fact that he shoots without apparent effort yet shoots his targets relatively quickly and efficiently.

Possibly one of the main advantages of maintained lead is that it forces the shooter to move correctly. The title of John Bidwell's book *Move, Mount, Shoot* encapsulates his system perfectly. Unlike swing through and point and swing, with John's method the gun doesn't start from behind the target or on it, but out in front of it. As John rightly puts it, the successful shot is the one who manages to get his gun the right distance ahead of the target more often than everyone else, and his method is designed to make this easier. Sounds simple enough, doesn't it, and in theory at least, at is. Let us look at the method in more detail.

When shooting Skeet judging the necessary forward allowance is relatively easy, since Skeet targets are the same the world over, The Skeet shooter knows, for example, that on station two low house his target will always break provided his gun is moving, and continues to move, 2–2½ feet ahead of it as he fires. Likewise on station five high

30 *George Digwood, one of the UK's leading Sporting shots, shows his method on a rabbit target*

house he knows that a lead of around 4 ft will result in a good break. But where does that leave the Sporting shooter, who by the definition of the game will not know the exact range of the targets with which he is confronted? John Bidwell believes that with practice this can be left to good technique, combined with natural hand and eye coordination. With practice and experience, he says, the shooter will learn instinctively to adjust the degree of forward allowance he gives a certain target.

A word of caution

Yet if the maintained lead method is such a recipe for success, why is it that so few shooting schools teach it, preferring instead the swing through system? There are a number of possible answers, not the least being that swing

through is undeniably easier to teach to a complete beginner, and UK shooting schools are in the main very traditional in their teaching methods. Maintained lead evolved with the Skeet discipline, and swing through had put down deep roots long before that game ever reached these shores. Also, a large number of shooting schools cater predominantly for game shooters, who are a quite different proposition to the clay shooter. The game shooter at the shooting school expects to be confronted with targets thrown at random in any direction. This, after all, is what happens on a game shoot. The shooter stands, as he must, favouring neither right nor left targets, which means he is facing forwards towards the source of the targets. If a target appears moving fast to his left or to his right his gun, because he is looking forward, is unavoidably pointing initially behind that target. He is compelled to start his swing from behind it. The school has little alternative but to teach a method that suits this shooting situation. To teach maintained lead would result in a most contrived style, and it would surely be ill-advised.

Clay shooting presents a quite different dimension, however, and one to which few of the long established shooting schools have adapted. As John Bidwell has proved, maintained lead works well in the right hands, but most schools don't and won't teach it.

John Bidwell's move, mount, shoot

Move . . .

The order of the words 'Move, Mount, Shoot' is very important, because very many shooters unwittingly reverse the first two and they 'Mount, Move, Shoot'. They see the target, mount their gun and then begin to move. Regardless of method this is fatal to good shooting! You must 'Move' first. This means that the swing begins while the gun is in the ready position, just fractionally before the gun mount begins. It is at this early stage of the shot that the top shooter relates his gun to the target. The swing at this stage is very much a turn of the body. The arms, moving with the body turn, simply raise the gun. They never swing independently.

Mount . . .

With the swing in motion the gun is brought smoothly to the correct fully mounted position, meaning that you make a moving gun mount. It is fair to say that this is one of the great secrets of any method of shooting, and observation of any top Sporting shooter will prove this fact. They all do it.

Shoot . . .

The gun is related to the target as the swing begins. The moving gun mount presents the gun to the target and once the gun is properly positioned in the shoulder and face the shot is fired without any further preamble. If the required lead has been correctly assessed then the target will break.

The foregoing probably sounds like solid support for the maintained lead method, and it is, but with reservations. John Bidwell uses it very successfully, but it must be born in mind that he has been shooting for very many years and therefore can take total gun control for granted. Maintained lead makes full control of the gun a prerequisite if it is to be used succesfully, and for this reason it is a debatable method for the beginner.

John Bidwell teaches his method to beginners from day one, and of course they benefit tremendously from personal coaching from the man himself. Arguably, though, the beginner working with another instructor would do well to learn the swing through method first, (he will probably have no choice) and learn it well. Certainly the move, mount, shoot progression should be employed regardless of method, never the mount, move, shoot so common to the average/ poor shooter. Once the lessons are well learnt and shooting begins to feel natural, then maintained lead is an option, and a good one.

8

FIFTY SPORTING – AN ACCOUNT

THE FOLLOWING is an account of how two friends competed in a fifty bird Sporting event at a well known shooting ground in the south of England. In order to avoid their embarrassment their names have been changed. The two work together, and while 27 year-old Dave has been shooting for ten years, and is a solid 'AA' class shot, 25 year-old Peter has only been shooting eighteen months and is striving to get out of 'C' class and into 'B'. Peter's style is quite good but he has trouble shooting the scores of which by now he feels he should be capable. Dave usually travels to shoots with two friends, one a 'AA' shooter like himself and the other an 'A' class man. For this event, though, he agreed to take Peter round what proved to be a fairly tricky course, to try to improve Peter's performance with some helpful advice. Dave knew the shooting ground well, and knew that when entries opened at 10.30 on Sunday morning the stands were usually quiet. So it was on this day, and Dave was able to help Peter without inconveniencing other shooters. They decided that Dave would shoot first and Peter would try to copy his example.

STAND ONE (fig. 7)

The first stand was four pairs. A fast 25 yd left to right orange rabbit was followed on report by a low rising incoming standard target. It came from directly ahead and flew slightly to the left of the shooting cage. 'I'm going to try to shoot the rabbit quite quickly' said Dave, 'and then the incomer should be easy.' Dave shot in his usual smooth style and managed to kill all eight.

On his first pair Peter missed the rabbit, and killed the second target well but late. 'Two things were wrong there' observed Dave. 'You pointed your gun right at the trap house before you called for the rabbit. This meant that you really had to chase hard in order to catch it. You then lifted your head from the stock just before you fired, and so you shot high as well as behind. Because you shot at the rabbit so late you had trouble getting on to that second target.' Dave then positioned Peter so that his gun was pointing a good 5 yd further out from the rabbit trap. 'As far out as that?'

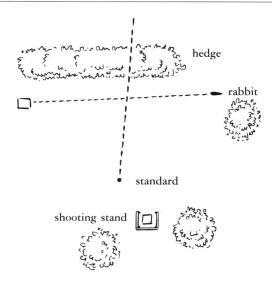

Fig. 7 *Fifty Sporting – stand one*

queried Peter. 'Yes' answered Dave, 'because even if you react as soon as you see the rabbit it will still pass your barrels. But nowhere near as much as when you pointed the gun at the trap! Now, what I want you to do is start to swing as soon as that rabbit appears. It will still overtake your gun, but not by much, and it will be easy to catch and swing through it. As soon as you've passed it, shoot. Keep swinging as you fire and keep your head glued to the stock.' Peter did as he was told and to his surprise he broke the rabbit much earlier than he would have thought possible. So soon did he break it he had lots of time for his second target. He swung too fast and missed in front. 'Don't say anything' said Peter, 'I know what I did.' His third pair he took perfectly. He held the gun well out from

31 *Stand one – a tricky rabbit and easy driven*

the trap as he'd been instructed and broke the rabbit as with the previous pair. He took his time with the incomer, swung smoothly and smoked it. The last pair got the same treatment and Peter came of the stand with a six on his card and feeling very pleased with himself.

STAND TWO (fig. 8)

The second stand was four pairs of very low simultaneous midis that quartered away right to left from a trap 15 yd to the side of the shooting cage. These were Peter's least favourite type of target. 'I always miss miles behind these' he said. Dave missed the first target of the pair but killed the second right in the middle of the pattern. 'I missed that target because I took the pair the wrong way round' Dave admitted. 'Where possible you should always take the rear target first, but I didn't and it's cost me a target.' He proceeded to demonstrate what he meant by smoking the remaining six targets. Seven scored.

Peter's first pair resulted in both targets being missed. 'There you are' he groaned, 'I always miss way behind these quartering birds.' 'Well, you didn't that time!' exclaimed Dave. 'You actually missed a good yard in front of both of them.' 'In front?' Peter sounded doubtful. 'Yes, in front! As with that rabbit on stand one, you pointed your gun much to close to the trap, and the targets were well down the field before you caught them. Your gun was moving much too fast as a result and to make matters worse you then gave them forward allowance.' Dave then positioned Peter so that his gun was pointing further out from the trap. 'Let the targets just pass the gun' Dave advised him, 'then catch the rear target and shoot right at it as you catch it'. Dave told Peter that he was then to transfer his gaze to the second target, catch that and again shoot right at it. 'But surely I'll shoot behind them, won't I?' Peter asked. 'Not if you keep the gun moving as you shoot.' Dave replied.

Peter felt uncomfortable with the gun

Fig. 8 *Fifty Sporting – stand two*

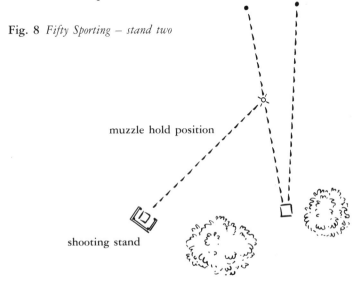

muzzle hold position

shooting stand

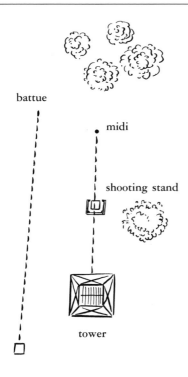

Fig. 9 *Fifty Sporting – stand three*

STAND THREE (fig. 9)

The third stand turned out to be the most difficult on the course, and there were five pairs to contend with! The first target was a wide battue which came from behind and twenty yards to the left of the shooting cage. It rolled over to show its face thirty yards out in front of the cage, dropping rapidly. The second target on report, a fast rising midi, came from a medium tower directly behind the cage and quickly disappeared behind some trees. 'Ten on here will be very difficult' stated Dave. 'You don't get much of a look at that first target, and the second is very awkward.' Dave took more time than usual setting himself for the pair, then called. He watched the edge-on battue carefully, following it with his muzzles, began mounting his gun just before the wafer-thin clay rolled over, then shot almost as soon as his gun hit his shoulder. The battue exploded. Dave immediately dropped the gun from his shoulder and into a high ready position, looking back for the second target. It was already on its way, and although he made what seemed to be a good swing the target flew on. 'I brought the gun back too far' Dave told Peter, 'and the target passed the muzzles and was under my gun. Once that happens it's very difficult to get onto its line.' For the second pair Dave made no mistake. He again dropped the gun quickly from his shoulder after breaking the battue, but made sure that his muzzles were under the tower target. A smooth mount

pointing what he thought was too far out, but he took his friend's advice. He shot the first target perfectly, but missed the second. 'You lost confidence on that second bird' noted Dave, 'and you shot way in front of it.' Peter nodded, surprised that he had hit the first one. As Dave had suggested he had shot right at it, and it had shattered! His third pair disappeared in two clouds of dust. His final pair was also killed, but he only just knocked the nose off the second target. 'You're right!' Peter declared. 'I shot right at that first target but gave the second some forward allowance, and nearly missed in front. That's really opened my eyes!' 'Well, you shot five of them,' smiled Dave, 'and that's a tricky little stand.'

32 Stand four – straightforward after the difficult stand three

and he broke the rapidly receeding mini in good style. He then broke the remaining three pairs and declared himself well satisfied. 'It would have been nice to have hit all ten but I would have settled for eight.'

Peter admitted to feeling overwhelmed by the stand, but Dave gave him some good advice. 'For someone at your present standard it's unrealistic to expect to hit all ten of these. I'm not saying you shouldn't try, but if I were you I would concentrate on hitting one from each pair and treat any double you manage to hit as a bonus.' Peter agreed that this made good sense, but admitted he had no idea how to tackle either target. 'This type of battue target is always fast and always dropping' said Dave. 'Although, like me, you shoot the swing through method this is the perfect target on which to use maintained lead.' Peter said that he had tried this method on some easy crossing targets and found it worked well. Dave told him to hold the gun well out on the flight line the target would take, then to start moving the gun ahead of it well before it rolled over. 'All I can say to you is give it plenty of lead and shoot well under its flight line. This way the target will drop into your pattern. But I won't pretend it's easy!' Peter agreed to see how he handled the battue and then make what he could of the high midi.

To both his and Dave's surprise he smoked the battue, dropped his gun from his shoulder then shot the midi in perfect style. 'Brilliant!' cried Dave. 'Do it again!' Sadly Peter missed the next pair, shooting over the battue and then mismounting his gun for the second.

'Don't take your eyes off that battue until you've shot at it' advised Dave. 'You were starting to look for that second bird before you had shot the first. Remember, on a very difficult pair like this it's better to hit one than miss two!' Peter took Dave's good advice, breaking the battue well but never really threatening the midi. He missed the battue in his fourth pair but picked up the second target perfectly. On his final pair it all came together and he broke them both in good style. Six scored. 'There will be 'A' and 'AA' shooters today who will come off this stand with worse scores than that' stated Dave. Peter agreed, and admitted that without Dave's steadying influence and good advice he could well have missed all of them.

STAND FOUR (fig. 10)

After the rigours of stand three stand four was quite straightforward. The shooter stood on a raised platform and the target emerged some 10 ft below his feet and flew straight away, rising steadily. He then got the same target on report. Dave positioned himself carefully and smoked all eight targets. He stayed up on the platform to watch how Peter would handle them. Peter broke the first target but missed the second. 'Your mistake there was to point the gun too high' said Dave, 'almost at the high point of the target's flight. Your gun wasn't moving at all, but you have to shoot this target with a moving gun because the target is rising quite steeply.' He positioned Peter's gun so that it was pointing about halfway out on the target's flight line. 'Now all you

Fig. 10 *Fifty Sporting – stand four*

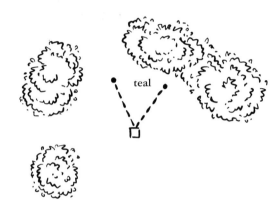

shooting stand

Fig. 11 *Fifty Sporting – stand five*

have to do is swing the gun up that line and shoot just as you pass the target. Then quickly drop the gun back to its original position and do the same again on the second target.' Following Dave's advice Peter proceeded to break his remaining three pairs with ease. 'That made all the difference' he said, delighted. Seven scored.

STAND FIVE (fig. 11)

The fifth stand was an old favourite, four pairs of simultaneous Springing Teal. They jumped up in true teal fashion some 25 yd ahead of the shooting stand, rising fast and no more than a few yards apart. Dave shot his first target on the rise, then carefully shot right at his second target as it slowed and

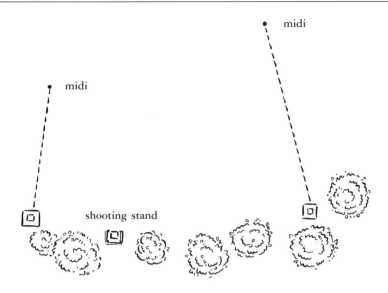

Fig. 12 *Fifty Sporting – stand six*

prepared to fall back. 'I would prefer to shoot both of them on the way up' he told Peter, 'but they are slowing down too quickly. To shoot them both rising would mean shooting too fast.' He broke the remaining three pairs in exactly the same fashion. Eight scored.

Peter was quietly confident on this stand, as Springing Teal were his favourite targets. His confidence was well placed, too, as he recorded his first straight stand of the day. Eight scored.

STAND SIX (fig. 12)

The final stand was tricky. The first target was a fast quartering away midi flying left to right from a low tower, which was positioned just to the left of the stand. This was followed by a standard target that flew right to left and away from another low tower, po-

sitioned some 30 yd to the right of the stand. The sides of the shooting cage prevented the second target being taken early, and this meant that it would probably have to be shot at a range approaching 40 yd.

'That second target is the hard one' Dave told Peter. 'I'm going to stand to favour that one and turn back in order to take the first.' Dave then demonstrated why he is in 'AA' class. He shot the first target out in front of the shooting cage, then quickly dropped the stock from his shoulder and brought the gun round to the right ready for the second target. As he had predicted, it was quite well out before he could shoot it, but a good smooth swing and follow through resulted in a dead centre hit in excellent style. He killed the other three pairs, too. 'That second target is dropping' he said, 'and I had to make a conscious effort to stay down on it.'

33 Stand five – springing teal

Peter stepped in to the cage, loaded his gun and prepared to call for his target. 'Hold it!' said Dave. 'You weren't watching what I did. If you stand to favour that first target you will never be able to pick up the second!' Dave got Peter to turn almost 90 degrees to the right. 'Now you can get at the second target. For the first target just pivot round so that your gun is about 15 yd out from the top of the tower. When you've shot your first bird just drop the gun out of your shoulder, turn and take your new hold position with the gun close to the right side of the cage.' Peter tried a few practice swings to get the feel of it, then took his first pair. He broke the first target well, but missed the second. 'I think I was behind it' he said. 'You were' Dave confirmed, 'and also you were several feet above it, too. You need to double your lead and remember to stay down on the bird.' Peter again hit the first target but missed the second. 'I know, I was still well behind it and above.' For his third pair everything went right and he broke both of them. 'I'm amazed how much forward allowance that sec-ond target needs!' he laughed. For his final pair he missed the first target but broke the second. 'I forgot all about that first target' Peter admitted, 'I was concentrating so hard on the second.' Five scored.

They totted up their scores, and Peter admitted to being delighted with his 37. 'If I had shot round on my own, or with my usual companions, I would have been lucky to break 30. What surprised me was that most of my problems were so easy to put right. It's not just how you shoot but how you manage yourself on each stand, the set up, and thinking exactly what you are trying to do before calling for the target. It's been a real lesson.' Dave was happy that he had been able to help Peter shoot a better score. 'I find that coaching someone like you does my own shooting a lot of good, too.' he said. 'It makes me think about it, and I'm sure I concentrate better as a result.' Later, Dave was also pleased to find that his 48 x 50 had won the shoot by a single target. The second place man, another 'AA' shooter, had lost all his targets on the dreaded stand three!

9

SKEET SHOOTING

SKEET – A BRIEF HISTORY

Origins

SKEET IS the most recently introduced of the three major disciplines, Trap, Sporting and Skeet.
Even so, it is hardly new. It started life
in the Twenties in the USA (34),
developing from a game invented by
some field shooters who were looking
to improve their performance at quail.
They bolted a clay trap to a tree stump,
scribed a circle of 25 yd radius around
it, and established 12 equidistant shooting stations on the circumference. The
fixed line clay was then shot from these
stations to give all angles at a variety of
ranges.

History does not record quite how
the intrepid trio protected the trapper,
but what is obvious is that this shooting 'round the clock', as it was known,
directed shot through a full 360
degrees. This became unpopular with a
neighbour, who reasonably claimed that
the regular impact of pellets on birds
was having an unsettling effect on his
chickens. To maintain the target angles
while protecting the hens, another trap

was installed some 42 yd from the
original, and pointing towards it, and
the shooters fired from stations on the
semi-circle connecting the two traps.

That the second trap happened to be
mounted several feet higher than the
first may have been coincidental, but
the idea remained. The game was discovered and publicized by two American outdoor magazines, and this created
quite a stir among the US shooting
fraternity. Unlikely as it now seems,
after just a few years what had started
as a bit of fun had grown into a full-
blown discipline. Until the advent of
this type of shooting there was no
alternative to Trap, and great game
though it is Trap offered none of the
variety of target angles presented by
the new discipline. Whereas Trap is very
much a game on its own – a clay version of a live target game that was itself
entirely artificial – clock shooting offered
a genuine form of practice for the field
shooter. It did not retain the name 'clock
shooting' for long, however. A maga-
zine competition for a suitable name for
this discipline came up with 'Skeet', a
derivation of a Scandinavian word for

shoot. Considering the game's origins it is perhaps fitting that it ended up with such a strange name! But this has one advantage: the disciplines Sporting and Trap find themselves translated into the language of the respective country in which they are shot. Skeet, having no meaning, is untranslatable and remains Skeet the world over.

Development of domestic Skeet
Inevitably, over the years the Skeet game has been gradually modified, although the actual field dimensions have remained the same. Not being based on

34 The youngest of the three major disciplines, Skeet has been around in various guises since its introduction in the USA in the Twenties. Station 6, English Skeet

anything in particular there was none of the restrictions placed on Skeet of the kind that limited Trap to a target or targets that always flew away from the shooter. In the game's founding country, the USA, Skeet had originally been based very much on the idea of shooting in the field. For the sake of realism target release was subject to a random delay following the shooter's call. Up to three seconds could elapse, and the shooter had to keep the gun down at the hip until the target emerged. Initially the doubles were released on report, but soon this was changed to a more difficult simultaneous release. The targets, which initially flew directly from one house to the other, were for safety reasons aimed out and away from the semi-circle of shooting stands. The targets crossed, and still do, 6 yd wide of station eight.

These rules made Skeet too difficult for the average shooter, however, and it was to this section of the shooting public that the new game originally appealed the most. Soon, the gun down rule was abandoned, and with it went the random delay. Target speeds were also slowed. Nowadays, the US National Skeet Shooting Association allows gun-in-the-shoulder shooting at targets that fly a maximum of 60 yd. At club level the targets fly just 55 yd. The game is still a challenge for the average shooter, but the experts nowadays shoot enormous scores.

Skeet arrived in the UK in the Thirties, and soon Great Britain was devising its own Skeet rules. As in the USA, these rules favoured easy scoring, and although there have been a number

35 *The ISU (Olympic) Skeet ready position. GB shooter, John Davidson, calls for a low house target*

of changes to the way Skeet is shot in the UK it remains a high scoring game. The domestic versions of Skeet are more popular with club and family shooters than the international version, which except at the highest level is too testing to be really enjoyable. The drawback of the domestic versions is that in major competitions the top shooters invariably find themselves in prolongued shoot-off events, which have been known to extend to 1,000 targets and more!

For a few years all the Skeet disciplines shared the same series of targets, with American NSSA Skeet and English Skeet being identical in all respects. English Skeet then went its own way, with different doubles and no station eight targets, while a major change to target sequence radically altered the international version, too.

ISU Skeet

The international version is Skeet shot under the rules of the International Shooting Union, the ISU (35). Although the discipline had been popular for many years it was not until 1968 that it first featured in the Olympic Games, in Mexico. With the host country having the option of introducing two new Olympic disciplines the Mexicans chose Skeet. This decision was prompted by the success of a Mexican lady shooter, Nuriah Ortiz, who earlier had achieved a fourth place in the senior event in the World Championships. She did not win an Olympic medal but nevertheless managed an honourable seventh place. Skeet had arrived.

In the current ISU version the targets must fly a minimum of 65m and a maximum of 67. The target release is subject to a random delay of from zero to three seconds, and the stock must touch the hip bone and remain there until the target emerges. With the exception of the target speed, which is now faster, ISU Skeet is very similar to Skeet as it was first shot in the USA back in the Twenties and Thirties. Arguably, if the game in the USA had persisted with the original rules, it would not have achieved its current high level of popularity. ISU Skeet is too difficult for it to be attractive to uncommitted international shooters. A good Sporting shooter can dip in and out of domestic Skeet and yet record great scores: not so with the ISU version.

SKEET: WHY SHOOT IT?

Sporting shooters can justifiably claim that their game is the most varied of the clay shooting sports, and many Sporting fans will never shoot any other discipline. The challenge for them is mastering the unknown. Trap shooters know exactly where their targets will come from, yet where they go is dependent on the vagaries of an auto varing trap machine or, as in the case of Five Trap or Olympic Trap, the instructions of a computer. Even so, the targets can only fly within certain prescribed limits. The shooter, through constant shooting, knows these limits and trains himself accordingly. The challenge of Trap is maintaining great concentration, controlling reflexes, and the repetition and application of good form to achieve high scores. But what of the Skeet shooter? He knows exactly where his target is coming from and exactly where it is going. He also knows its height and its speed. He does not have the great variation of the Sporting shooter nor the uncertainty of the Trap shooter. But the apparent repetitiveness of Skeet can be deceiving. Undoubtedly, if all 25 targets were shot from the same station then the game would be very boring indeed. Yet although each individual round is identical to each and every other round, the challenge is presented by the constantly changing target angles presented on each station. At first glance Skeet should be a walkover, yet maddeningly it rarely is, even for the very best shooters. Particularly at ISU Skeet, each round is a whole new experience, and anyone who thinks differently should try it.

SKEET SHOOTING METHODS

In the course of a major Skeet championship a keen observer will see all three methods of shooting in evidence. Without doubt, though, maintained lead is by far the most popular of the three, with point and swing a distant second. Indeed, Skeet shooting might have been a discipline invented with maintained lead in mind. For many shooters maintained lead works best at relatively close ranges, and on targets of known speed, height and direction. No Skeet target is taken beyond 25 yd, and most are shot a good deal closer.

The maintained lead shooter, if he is any good, can easily be spotted on the Skeet range. He is the one for whom the targets seem slower, who appears to shoot his targets early but without rushing. It is fair to say that this is the method used by most leading Skeet shooters the world over.

Skeet methods in the UK

Despite the large number of top Skeet shooters who favour maintained lead, there are still many who successfully employ the other two methods. Among them is one of the UK's most successful campaigners on the international Skeet circuit, Joe Neville. For a number of years Neville was the only serious ISU Skeet shot in these islands, one of the few men who shot the discipline to the exclusion of all else. His commitment extended to building his own Skeet range, although finances were such that he was obliged in the early days to use any cartridge he could lay his hands on. He carefully studied the form of the opposition and closely questioned all the leading shooters and coaches of his day as to how they achieved the scores they did, then went away and worked at it. He achieved excellent results at the highest level, and with a little more luck might well have carried off the Olympic Skeet gold medal in 1972 in Munich. A poor seventh round dropped him from the leading position, and in the end three shooters tied on 195, with Joe a tantilizing one target behind on 194. His fine example prompted others to follow his dedicated and single-minded approach, and these days there is a hard core of UK international shooters of world class who owe a great deal to his early example.

Although officially retired from competition, Joe Neville's great experience and expertise is being put to good use. He is now the British team coach, and is helping many shooters achieve their full potential. Very much a self-taught shooter, Joe has subsequently spent many valuable hours with foreign shooting teams, learning their coaching methods. Along with his own accumulated knowledge this extra input has allowed the British team to make great progress.

Maintained lead Skeet

It was the adoption of this method that transformed the author of this book, Paul Bentley, from a good ISU Skeet shot to a very good one!

Another successful early advocate of this method of shooting was Jim Sheffield (38). Having absorbed it during a period when he lived and worked in North America, Sheffield first applied it to English Skeet. Almost all American shooters use maintained lead for shooting Skeet, and Jim had great success with it when he returned to the UK. Inevitably he brought the method to ISU Skeet, a discipline in which his determination and skill soon saw him performing as a world class member of the Great Britain team.

Although now very popular, the maintained lead method is misunderstood by many shooters, who get themselves in a tangle when they try to employ it. This is partly due to the misleading name, maintained lead. This seems to imply that the gun is moved carefully along at a fixed distance ahead

36 *Great Britain Team shooter, Ken Harman, shoots maintained lead Skeet from an American-style crouch*

The Neville method

Joe Neville's method is based on 'point and swing', modified to suit the special demands of Skeet, and specifically ISU Skeet. Anyone who has watched Joe shoot could not fail to be impressed by his smooth, controlled style (37). He always seems to have plenty of time, and shoots the targets as quickly and efficiently as you could wish. Yet he eschews the concept of conscious forward allowance, 'feet and inches shooting' as he calls it, and this is where his method differs from 'point and swing' as taught by the CPSA. The CPSA 'method' requires the shooter to point the muzzles at the target as he brings the gun to his shoulder in a moving gun mount. There is then a conscious swinging away from the target to establish the correct lead picture, and the shot is fired with the muzzles still being moved away ahead of the target.

With Joe Neville's method forward allowance is almost entirely instinctive and automatic, with the shooter firing almost 'at' the target with an accelerating gun. In a way this reflects the thinking behind Robert Churchill's somewhat controversial 'no lead' method. But whereas Churchill advocated this method for targets of all ranges Neville is concerned only with the fast and close targets of ISU Skeet. It is at just this type of target that the Churchill method works best.

Having said that, Joe is quite aware that forward allowance is essential for nearly all Skeet Targets, although the degree of conscious allowance with his method is minimal. For the method to work well it must be accepted that the approach to high house targets is slightly different to those from the low house. A right-handed shooter will always swing less freely when turning to the right than when moving in the opposite direction. To compensate for this Neville advises the shooter to feel that the gun has pushed more ahead of the high house target before the shot is fired. This is not the same as giving a deliberate lead of so many feet: the gun accelerates ahead and the shot is fired without hesitation. The low house target, moving right to left, needs less apparent 'push through'.

The advantage of this approach is that the shooter can feel that he is shooting almost right at each target, allowing the swing to supply much of the necessary forward allowance. This makes the approach to each target much the same, without the need for a different lead for each one. Joe's method will work as long as the shooter accelerates the gun, and continues to do so throughout the shot. In his words:

'I try to move the gun as close to the target as I can at the beginning of the shot. Then as long as I concentrate on the target the gun will automatically accelerate as I'm mounting it. Firing the gun is a matter of instinct. As soon as the gun beds into position the shot is fired. That's all there is to it.'

37 *Perfect balance and control, Joe Neville style. For many years one of the world's finest ISU Skeet shots, Joe is now the Great Britain Team coach*

38 For a perfect example of maintained lead ISU Skeet you need look no further than Great Britain Team shooter, Jim Sheffield

of the target, with an almost rifle type aim being used. Shooters imagine that they must look simultaneously at gun and target, although they soon find that in practice this is quite impossible. You cannot focus on a gun that is quite literally at the end of your nose and at the same time hold sharp focus on a target that might be as much as 25 yd away. Eyes do not work like that. Although initially a more calculated method than that used by Joe Neville, maintained lead is still very much dependent on instinctive shooting based on hand and eye coordination.

The major misunderstanding occurs in the very earliest part of the maintained lead swing. Knowing that a certain lead picture is necessary in order

for a given target to break, the shooter makes the mistake of trying to establish that gun/target relationship as soon as the target appears. This can not be done! To do that the shooter would have to accelerate the gun instantly to match the speed of the target, while at the same time perfectly judging the lead picture. Apart from other considerations, such as unworldly reflexes, such a swing would defy the laws of physics.

Correctly done the maintained lead swing is almost a reversal of that required to shoot either the 'swing through' system or 'point and swing'. There is no attempt to adjust the lead immediately the gun starts to move. Instead the gun is held quite well out from the trap house and the swing is set in motion as the target appears. At this point in the swing the gun is too far in front of the target, perhaps several yards, but the eye is always focussed

Skeet the 'swing through' way (3a)

This is surely the more difficult way to shoot Skeet, especially the international version. One of the few UK shooters ever to shoot consistent world class ISU Skeet scores using 'swing through' was Wally Sykes. To say this method did not work for Wally would be a denial of his genius as an all-round shooter. And this is where his success with the method largely lay. Wally could shoot any discipline he chose, and to a very high standard. His successes as a Skeet shooter are well enough known to those who were around in the Seventies and Eighties, but many forget that before these achievements went into the record book he had won the European FITASC Sporting championship. He was also well nigh unbeatable in multi-discipline events. During these events he would often be High Gun at the Trap disciplines, much to the chagrin of the Trap shooters, and then with those out of the way he would mop up in the Skeet and Sporting events and take the top prize. His great secret was this: whatever he might have lacked in copybook technique, Wally always had the ability to get the gun on to the target.

Not even a shooting genius like Wally Sykes' however, could make 'swing through' at ISU Skeet look anything but hard work. He would point his gun almost into the target exit hole, and when the target emerged he would make a long raking swing to catch it. Less talented shooters, using 'maintained lead' or 'point and swing', would break their target over the centre peg. Wally would break his target just as effectively, but several yards later. On doubles this usually meant Wally then had to swing very fast to get back in time for that second target, and in unfavourable conditions he would often break the target only a yard or so before the boundary marker. He shot many great scores in this fashion, yet in the hands of someone with less skill the method was a non-starter. Yet with the exception of Joe Neville, Jim Sheffield and this book's editor it is likely that 95 per cent of all UK Skeet shooters shot this way until well into the Eighties.

39 *Many English Skeet shooters shoot the swing-through method*

hard on the target and never the gun. Because the acceleration of the gun is smooth and gradual the target, in the initial stages of the swing, actually begins to catch the muzzles. This is a complete reversal of what happens when shooting 'point and swing' or 'swing through', where the gun swings away from the target. Of course, the gun very quickly accelerates to match the pace of the target. During the final quarter of the 'maintained lead' swing the muzzles are moving at the same speed as the target, and ahead of it. As the gun beds into the shoulder and face the shot is fired without any hesitation. Throughout the shot the eye is fixed only on the target.

Those who criticise this method might ask: 'If you don't look at the gun how do you know that it is pointing the right amount in front of the target? How do you know where the gun is relative to the target?' Similar questions could be asked of tennis players or golfers: how do they know where their racquets or clubs are during a shot? The answer is that through constant practice they learn by feel. They certainly do not have to look at the racquet or club, and to try to do so would produce some very strange shots.

The maintained lead method would seem to require excellent timing, as well as fine hand and eye coordination, if it is to work properly, and indeed it does. But so do all methods of shooting a

40 A South Korean ISU Skeet shooter with the much copied USA crouch. Despite the strain on the knee joints some shooters find it helps then shoot more aggressively

shotgun. Without these vital ingredients no method will work. Yet regular practice soon has the maintained lead method under control, but only when the basic idea is fully understood. Once learned it is a very strong method for shooting Skeet.

THE BASICS OF GOOD SKEET SHOOTING

The absolute basics of good Skeet shooting are the same as for all shotgun shooting. There are, however, certain basics that apply specifically to Skeet, or which need particular emphasis. Skeet is a discipline of repetition: for instance the targets are the same the world over. This is not to say that that target will necessarily fly down exactly the same track time after time: wind, weather and

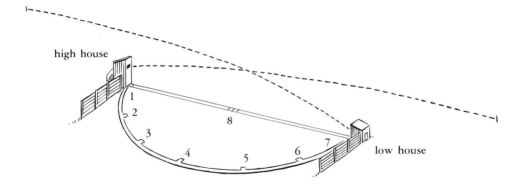

Fig. 13 *Skeet range*

the slight variations allowable within the rules prevent that. Yet each target will always fly within closely defined limits, and should one stray outside these limits it is ruled a 'No bird'. This consistency allows the Skeet shooter to train for each and every target that he will encounter in a round, confident that he will not receive any surprises other than those caused by the weather.

Stance

There are some strange stances to be seen at almost any Skeet shoot, including international events. Some shooters crouch down low, others lean forward at seemingly impossible angles (40). Some stand with their feet very far apart, others throw their weight about so much they fall off the stand after almost every shot. Confusingly, for those hoping to find good examples to copy, some of these strange stances belong to quite creditable performers! Yet it is fair to say that in many of these cases the performances achieved are despite the

odd stances and not because of them.

For all shotgun shooting it is the targets that help define the stance. A high target will require the shooter to bend, either straight back or as he turns. A very low target, possibly flying well below the level of the feet, will require a distinct lean forward. The terms 'High target' and 'Low target' at Skeet have little to do with elevation, referring only to the fact that a given target has emerged from the high or low house. By any standards both targets are low. The high house trap is only 10 ft above the ground, the low house $3\frac{1}{2}$ ft, and both targets cross in the centre some 15 ft from the ground. They are actually very similar flat targets flying at more or less the same speed. It is a fact that if the shooter on any station mounts his gun correctly while standing nearly erect, his muzzles will be practically at the right elevation for any Skeet target with the exception of station eight. In short, unless the shooter is trying to make life difficult for himself, a normal erect stance is ideal. For perfect examples look no further than the Czechs, or the Russians, or the teams that used to represent what was East Germany – no frills, no fuss – upright stance, call, turn smoothly as the gun mounts, bang. It is so simple when you watch it, yet some people seem unable to absorb the lesson.

Foot position

A narrow stance makes it easier to swing, but a wide stance gives better stability. Split the difference and stand just wide enough for stability. For most of us this means feet no more than shoulder width apart. Where your feet point will determine how easily you swing, and the diagram is a good indicator of the best way to stand on each station. Generally, on any given station, you should stand facing the point where you will break the second target of the double from that station. The logic behind this is simple. In doubles the first target is always taken quickly, usually as or before the target reaches the centre peg. The shooter winds-up slightly during the taking of the first target, then unwinds again as he takes the second. Any slight restriction created when taking the first target in this fashion is not a problem. Try standing to favour the first target when taking doubles, however, and the second target will be frequently missed as the swing binds up. Where there is no double then stand facing the break point of the individual target. By standing to favour the target break-point you will create a slight spring effect when you bring the gun round to your ready position.

Ready position

Whether you choose to start with the gun in your shoulder, slightly dismounted or, because the rules demand it, right down on the hip ISU style, there is one factor that must be observed if you hope to be consistent. In the ready position the barrels must be exactly perpendicular to the eye (41). Shooters who struggle on one particular station will often find that the problem can be traced to this misalignment in the ready position. Only when the gun is directly beneath the master eye is it related to where that eye is looking (**fig. 14**). If the barrels are off-set from this eyeline, most often to the right of perpendicular, then the gun will not be pointing where the shooter imagines it to be. One of the major causes of this problem is a poor

41 *With his quicksilver shooting style, top Sporting shot, Mickey Rouse, is also a whizz at English Skeet! Note his narrow stance and upright position*

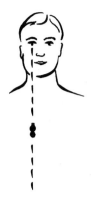

the barrels should align directly under the eye at address

Fig. 14 *Shooting Skeet – correct alignment of eye and barrel*

stance, particularly one that leans over to one side or the other. In fact the gun's misalignment is only corrected once the stock beds into the shoulder and face, and it is only then, as the shot is fired, that the shooter realizes all is not well! This sort of miss is very frustrating, because the shot may feel perfect as the gun is being brought to the shoulder, yet just as the gun beds into position the whole thing seems to go wrong. If this description sounds familiar to you, then check on the perpendicular position of those barrels.

Barrel position

Regardless of how you position the gun at address there is one golden rule: always hold the muzzles so that they are level with or slightly below the target flight line. If the muzzles are held above the line there will be a tendency for the muzzles to dip as the stock is brought to the shoulder, causing a miss below the target. Holding the muzzles

below the target flight line has the reverse effect, and also makes it difficult to relate the gun to the target.

Where to look

More appropriate would be to subtitle this section 'Where not to look'. Many Skeet shooters make the mistake of looking directly into the target exit slot. Because they are staring into a black hole the target is often quite some way out before they see it. Much better is to look slightly out of the chute, perhaps a yard or so, on the target's flight line. If a soft focus is held here, one that is focussed on nothing in particular, then the eyes will fasten onto the target as soon as it appears.

On station two high bird the eyes should be allowed to look even further out, perhaps midway between gun and high house. To look closer to the exit hole than this means turning the head out of position, and this can lead to a poor gun mount.

A ROUND OF SKEET

The preparation for a round of competitive Skeet starts before you walk onto station one and load your gun. Unless you shoot the entire event on one Skeet field, highly unlikely even in a minor competition, then the targets on each field are likely to be different to the others, however slightly. Important variations include visibility, susceptibility to weather conditions and target speed.

Visibility

Black targets stand out well against the sky but are very hard to see against a dark background. The opposite applies

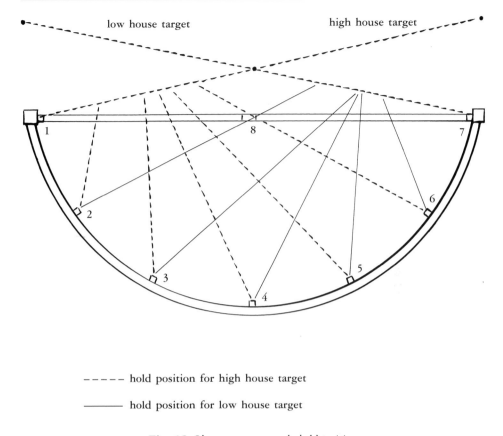

low house target   high house target

- - - - - hold position for high house target

————— hold position for low house target

Fig. 15 *Skeet range – muzzle hold positions*

to coloured targets. Some shooting grounds have perfectly clear backgrounds on certain Skeet fields, while their other field or fields have a wood out in front. Obviously, under these circumstances, visibility will change from field to field, and it is only by familiarizing yourself with each field, and noting the differences, that you will properly prepared.

42 *Not to be confused with his Sporting namesake, former Great Britain Team shooter, Stuart Clark, shows fine style on a station 5 double*

Weather

A field shielded by trees will throw quite different targets to one exposed to the elements. Have a good look at the squad shooting in front of you and note what happens to their targets. It is too late to discover that the high target is diving as it leaves the trap when you have just missed your first target out! At one European championship in Italy a full gale was blowing left to right across the fields. So high was the wind that national flags were beginning to shred on their flagpoles. Every high target was diving almost to the ground only yards beyond the centre peg. Even at this level of experience many shooters failed to see this target when shooting doubles until it was too late. They were looking for the target in its usual spot in the sky, but it was out of sight below their barrels. Some shooters even opened their guns having fired at the low house target, believing the high target had not been thrown. These were costly errors that most shooters avoided by judicious observation prior to their round. In very tricky conditions the shoot was still won with a score of 198 × 200.

Target speed

Although Skeet targets are supposed to conform to regulations governing speed this is no guarantee that each field will be identical. If the targets of one field are a yard or two short of the minimum distance while another has targets flying a yard or two beyond the maximum, then the difference in speed is quite significant. Once the targets are set for the day there is nothing that can be done: they certainly won't be altered. By noting the variation you can take the appropriate step of slightly altering your normal muzzle hold position to suit the target speed.

Station by station hold and shooting positions (fig. 15)

By referring to the diagrams you can see the suggested hold positions for each station, as well as the spot where each target should be broken. These apply for both domestic and international Skeet. Despite the variation in target angle from station to station the shooting rhythm for each target should be exactly the same. This applies equally to the doubles. Someone listening to the shooting ought not to be able to tell whether you are shooting a pair on station one, station four or station seven: the rhythm for all is exactly the same.

10

*T*RAP
SHOOTING

TRAP – A BRIEF HISTORY

TRAP SHOOTING is the senior competitive shotgun game, having been around in one form or another for many years. On a world-wide basis it is certainly the most popular of all the clay disciplines. There are several Trap shooting disciplines, all of them sharing one major feature: targets that go away from the shooter at a variety of angles.

Trap shooting evolved from live pigeon shooting. The unfortunate pigeons were held captive in five collapsible boxes, or traps, and any one of the five would be released when, at the shooter's command, a wire was pulled. Live pigeon shooting is banned in most countries nowadays, but the clay versions are still called Trap and most shooters still use 'Pull!' to call for their targets. Wires are no longer pulled, however: most Trap targets are released electrically or electronically.

Moral issues aside, live pigeons presented a considerable challenge to the shooter by virtue of their jinking flight. The modern Trap shooter does not have

an awkward live target to deal with since his clays fly straight and true. The difficulty for him lies in the speed of the target and its unknown angles. The ultimate Trap game, Olympic Trap, features very fast targets that vary greatly in height and angle, as well as speed.

GUN MOUNT

The targets used for all Trap disciplines are 110 mm standards, although they can be of any colour to suit the background. Depending on the Trap discipline the shooter is positioned about 16 yd behind the point where the target emerges. The target is released the instant the shooter calls 'Pull!', and even at the mild speed of Down the Line the target will travel 10 yd or so before the shooter reacts. This means that the target will be shot at a minimum range of some 25 yd, and for this reason Trap shooters call for their targets with the gun already mounted. Initially, many newcomers to the Trap disciplines find this aspect difficult to come to terms with, especially if they are familiar with Sporting or Skeet. Starting with the gun in the shoulder feels very unnatural.

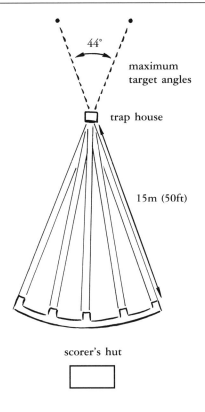

44°

maximum
target angles

trap house

15m (50ft)

scorer's hut

Fig. 16 *Down the line layout*

Attempting to shoot with the gun dis-mounted will hit some targets, but ul-timately gun in the shoulder is the only method worth pursuing.

MAJOR TRAP DISCIPLINES

Down the Line (fig. 16)
Down the Line is a high scoring Trap discipline with a tremendous following in the UK (43). The gently rising tar-gets fly at a fixed elevation angle, while an unreadable auto-angling trap varies the target angle 22 degrees either side of centre. The target flies between 50–55 yd, with the shooters positioned on five stations 16 yd behind the traphouse.

A target like this is easy to hit even for a relative novice, and with two shots allowed at each target it would seem even easier. There is a catch, however. A points system awards three for a first barrel kill and two for a second, and it is points rather than kills that determ-ine the winner of a competition. Thus a shooter hitting 90 targets with his first barrel, and missing ten completely (270 points, written 90/270) will beat another shooter who having hit all 100 targets has used a second shot for each (200 points, written 100/200). This actual result is highly unlikely, but it does illustrate the points system.

The question: 'Why would anyone want to shoot relatively easy targets' supplies its own answer. The possibility of a high score is part of the attraction, yet the highest score, 100/300, is far from guaranteed even for the most expert shooter. And, of course, however easy the discipline the winning is just as difficult.

Nearly all of the leading UK inter-national Trap shooters cut their teeth on DTL, many of them, like Kevin Borley, being star performers before moving on to the more testing Trap disciplines.

Automatic Ball Trap
ABT is similar in concept to DTL in that a single automatic trap is used to launch the target and the shooters fire from one of five stations. ABT, though, has the extra element of variable eleva-tion and the possible target angles are

43 DTL has a tremendous following in the UK. Here Andy King shows the way

44 *Leading Olympic Trap shooter, Peter Boden, having a change of scene at the ABT British Grand Prix*

greater, too. Add target speed that is half as fast again as DTL and you have a game that is considerably more testing (44).

ABT, though, has nothing like the following of DTL. It is a discipline that falls rather between two stools, having neither the easy scoring attractiveness of DTL nor the subtle difficulty of Olympic Trap or Universal Trench. It is, however, a fine stepping stone between DTL and the sterner international Trap disciplines, and provides excellent practice for these games when a UT or OT layout is not available. Like these two disciplines the scoring is kills to count, so whether you hit your target with the first or the second barrel the score is the same: one point.

One of the drawbacks of ABT is that the rules allow considerable flexibility in the lateral and vertical angles that may be set for a competition. A 'soft' ABT layout might be only a little more testing than DTL, whereas a layout using the maximum elevation variation and widest permited angles presents a far greater challenge. Unfortunately, too many grounds, knowing that shooters like to break targets, take the soft option. They do neither the shooter, who is fooled as to his true ability, nor the game, which is diminished, any favours.

The other drawback with ABT is the random nature of the targets. It is quite possible for one shooter on a squad to get a high proportion of hard-angled targets while another gets rather softer and easier angles. This potential unfairness is what prevented ABT from being considered as a serious option to Olympic Trap.

Universal Trench

Universal Trench, or Five Trap as most of its followers refer to it, is the FITASC version of Olympic Trap. It employs five fixed line traps, positioned at varying heights, angles and speeds, and five shooting stations. It does not have the target variety of Olympic Trap nor does it have the same universal following. A

major Five Trap event will possibly have six or seven participating nations, whereas an Olympic Trap world championship event will often have 40 or more.

Olympic Trap

Often called the Blue Riband of clay shooting, Olympic Trap is the most testing of the many Trap disciplines. Five banks of three traps provide the 15 trap layout with enough variety in target speed, elevation and direction to test the very best Trap shooters to the limit. It is a discipline where only the shooter in tip top condition, both physically and mentally, can hope to produce high scores. As with all the international Trap games it is scored kills to count, with a first or second barrel kill counting as one point.

BASIC TRAP SHOOTING TECHNIQUE

The gun mount

Many shooters new to Trap get the wrong idea about the role of the gun mount in Trap shooting. It is as important to be able to mount the gun in one smooth movement when shooting Trap as it is when shooting Sporting or Skeet, yet many Trap shooters spend several seconds juggling the gun around in their shoulder and adjusting their head position before settling and calling for the target. This takes all the feel out of the shot and makes it far too studied. Most of the leading Trap shooters hold the gun in a low ready position, then mount it in one smooth movement and call for the target without further ado.

Smooth gun mount

Leading British Olympic Trap shooter, Kevin Gill, attributes much of his success in recent years to changing to a smoother gun mount. Before the change he would fiddle about with the gun in his shoulder, taking great pains and no little time, getting everything just so. After settling there would be a period of a several seconds for contemplation before he finally called for the target. Sometimes he shot well, sometimes not so well. The change when it came was total. He schooled himself to mount the gun in one smooth movement and to call as soon as the gun firmed into his shoulder. The result was a shooting style that is very consistent, and it has led to some great victories at the highest level (45a–b). His style is now much easier on the eye, too!

45a–b Top Olympic Trap shooter, Kevin Gill, in action. Already a leading shot, he cut his pre-call preparation time in half and found immediate improvement

The Trap stance

Although there are always those who are unorthodox, the vast majority of successful Trap shooters take a narrow stance with the heels no more than 8 in apart. Relative to the gun-hold the foot positions are as follows: the leading foot points to one o'clock while the rear foot points to three o'clock. This allows the shooter to turn freely in all directions while maintaining good balance. Weight just favours the forward foot.

While it is possible to shoot the occasional target at DTL and even ABT using the sustained lead method the only method worth serious consideration is swing through. Even granted ultra fast reflexes the Trap shooter will usually find that his target is out and flying away from his gun. It will be either rising and straight away, or heading to the left or to the right. Not knowing where his target is going until it is on its way he has no option but to wait until he sees it. He must then swing his gun after the target and swing through it.

Knowing how to look for the target is one of the secrets of good Trap shooting. With the gun in the shoulder it is too easy to focus on the rib or the bead, and this means the target is, at best, only seen as a blur. Once the gun is properly mounted it should then be ignored. The eyes must look into the space where the target must fly. This means expanding the vision to cover quite a large area, especially at the fast international disciplines. Obviously the eyes cannot focus on this large area, and indeed must be allowed to look but without seeing, holding what might

best be described as a soft focus on nothing in particular. Then, when the target emerges, it will be immediately picked up by the eyes. For the first few yards of its flight it will be a blur, but a blur which rapidly resolves into a sharply focussed target. At this point the gun is set in motion, accelerating along the target's line of flight. The shot is fired as the gun catches and passes the target.

A very important point, applicable to all clay disciplines, is that the shooter moves 'as a piece' with the gun. Any independent movement of the gun

46 Jackie Field showing good DTL form

47 England DTL international Neville Bailey

means that the gun mount position must alter, and when that happens the eye-gun-target relationship is spoilt and the shot will probably be missed.

Forward allowance

The nature of the swing at Trap – an accelerating one from behind and through the target – largely eliminates any need for conscious forward allowance, or lead, even at the widest international Trap targets. On the quick and wide international targets any extra lead required is granted by the faster swing.

Fig. 17 *Shooting DTL*

Ask most proficient Trap shooters how much lead they give a particular target and most will answer: 'None!' This is not to say that no lead is necessary – lead is a factor on all steeply rising and angled targets – but there is no conscious lead. The speed of the swing takes care of that.

Good Trap shooting is the perfect example of conditioned reflexes at work. The shooter sees his target, swings his gun up the flight line and shoots without hesitation right at the target as he passes it. It is pure reflex action. Leading British Olympic Trap shooter Peter Croft encapsulates the ideal Trap shooting method: 'See it and shoot it.'

The second barrel

If the first shot is directed by pure reflex than the second is more of the same. The second barrel is fired when the first shot is missed, and this means the target is quite well out at DTL and a long way out at Olympic Trap. There is no time for anything fancy: the shooter's eyes must be rivetted to the target, and the shooter has just a short moment to

get the muzzles onto the target flight line. The shot is again fired without any hesitation. Newcomers will often be mystified to see shooters firing a second shot at the pieces of a target that has already been well broken. This is not showing off, although there is a certain satisfaction in 'smoking' a small piece of target that is spinning away. The real purpose of it, though, is to keep the second barrel reflexes up to scratch, an important factor when the shooter is breaking nearly every target with his first barrel.

SHOOTING DTL (fig. 17)

The basic shooting method applies to all the Trap disciplines, but DTL is unique in that the trap is positioned in a small house above ground level rather than in a pit. Some DTL shooters hold their gun muzzles dead centre on the trap house roof regardless of the peg they are shooting from. Many others adjust their gun point position relative to the top of the Trap house according to the peg from which they are shooting. These muzzle hold positions are on or just above the traphouse roof as follows:

- Peg one: the left edge
- Peg two: midway between the left edge and the centre
- Peg three: dead centre
- Peg four: midway between the centre and the right edge
- Peg five: the right edge

The reason these hold positions vary is due to the nature of the target angles. From peg one the shooter receives only straight or left angled targets, while from peg five the shooter has straight or right angled targets to contend with. Moving the muzzle hold position across the trap house roof as the shooter progresses from peg to peg allows him to take advantage of these limited target angles.

The stance is aligned to favour these hold positions. On peg one the stance is aligned on a point several yards left of the gun hold position. On peg two the stance is just left of the gun hold position. On peg three the stance is straight, on peg four it is aligned slightly right of centre and several yards right on peg five.

As with all clay shooting, it is very important to concentrate fully at all times. This is especialy true where high scoring disciplines are concerned, because it is all too easy when shooting well to begin thinking of the possible score. If there is a secret it is to shoot one target at a time. Forget those that have gone before and those that are to come: if 100 straight is a distinct possibility do not spoil it by letting your mind wander to the award ceremony!

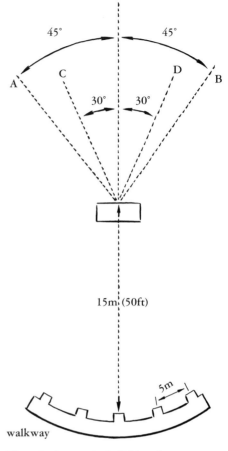

Fig. 18 *Automatic Ball Trap layout*

SHOOTING ABT (fig. 18)

The similarities between DTL and ABT are apparent but limited. As many have observed, ABT is like DTL gone mad! A single automatic machine is employed, but whereas the DTL trap varies only its angles the ABT machine also varies its elevation. Target speed is far greater too, a 80 yd rocket as opposed to a 52 yd lob. The elevation varies from daisy cutter to steeply climbing, and because of the low level target the trap has to be buried in a pit. The target therefore emerges at ground level, like

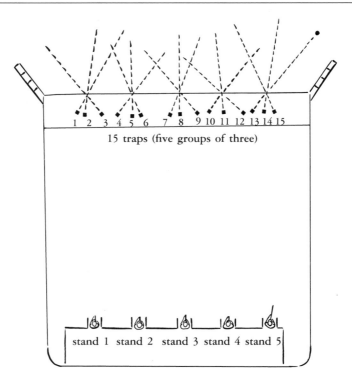

Fig. 19 *Olympic Trap layout viewed from above*

Olympic Trap and Five Trap. As with DTL most ABT shooters hold the muzzles to the left or right of the trap position according to the peg they are shooting from.

The height the muzzles are held above the trap house is determined by the elevation of the lowest possible target. Holding the muzzles a foot or more above the house gives some advantage on sharply rising targets, but when the low one zips out it can easily go a long way before the shooter sees it. For this reason most shooters hold the muzzles right on the trap house, sometimes even slightly below it.

SHOOTING OLYMPIC TRAP (fig. 19)

Olympic Trap is the ultimate Trap discipline, a fast and exciting clay game that tests eye and hand coordination to the maximum. Unlike DTL or ABT the traps employed are fixed line, but there are 15 of them and they are set up with high difficulty value in mind. Each of the five shooting stands has a bank of three traps arranged in front of it, but below ground. The targets appear from ground level and skim away low, rise quite steeply, and everything in between. The left trap of the three points somewhere to the right, the right trap somewhere to the left, and the middle trap either straight or slightly left or right of straight. This arrangement means that the three targets emerge from about the same point in front of the shooter. Needless to say, each bank of three traps is different in angle speed and elevation to the other four banks. Throw in variable target speeds and you have a recipe for a clay discipline that is totally absorbing. Target release is by acoustically-activated electronics, and this gives targets that are on their way almost before the shooter has completed the command: 'Pull!' The instantaneous release and high target speed means that the timing of the shot is critical. Two shots are allowed per target, and very few 25 straights are ever achieved without the second barrel being brought into play.

Cartridges

For many years Olympic Trap rules allowed 28g cartridges, and when this was reduced to 26g many shooters were convinced scores would suffer alarmingly. Surprisingly, scores actually improved. In the late Eighties shot loads were again reduced, this time to 1oz Fears that this reduction would be the undoing of Olympic Trap shooters again

proved groundless, although it took some time for shooters to adjust to the new load. The further reduction to 24 g may at last make Olympic Trap too difficult, although in the light of previous experience it would be rash to say that scores will suffer for certain. Without doubt, though, such a small shot charge will call for great accuracy.

Gun hold

The shooting technique for Olympic Trap is basically the same as for all Trap disciplines: a narrow stance, weight slightly favouring the forward foot, and a pre-mounted gun. The gun hold position is something for individual experiment, although a good starting point is right at the mark where the targets emerge (**fig. 20**). This allows full view of the target from the moment it appears. Some shooters point their gun up to a foot or more above this mark, however. This can give them something of a running start at most targets, but one obvious drawback is that low targets can be several yards out before they come into view.

Focus

Regardless of where you point the gun it is vital that you see and focus the

Fig. 20 *Olympic Trap viewed from the side*

target as soon as you can. This is impossible if you focus either on the gun or on the target exit mark. Your eyes must first unfocus before finding and refocussing the target. The target will be gone in a flash, a blur of colour that will not come into focus until the target has travelled a long way. The proper place to look is nowhere in particular! A good expression to bear in mind is 'expand your vision', since this describes it perfectly. Having mounted the gun point it at your hold position then allow the eyes to go slightly out of focus, thus viewing a large area out in front of the traps. Then, whether the target goes straight, left or right it must fly through this softly viewed area and your eyes will lock onto it and focus it almost immediately. This is the moment to begin swinging the gun. By moving only when the target is focussed you will ensure that the gun starts off on exactly the right line, whereas chasing a blur can often mean the gun moving on the wrong line and at the the wrong speed. Once the gun is moving the shot becomes very much a matter of conditioned reflex action. With your eyes focussed hard on the target the gun is swung through the target and the shot is fired immediately. There is

definitely no time to check that everything is perfect before firing! Just swing and trust to natural eye and hand coordination to time the shot properly.

The second barrel

No one is perfect, and even the finest Olympic Trap shooter will occasionally miscue and miss with his first barrel. At this stage the target will be at least 30 yd away, probably nearer 35. Ten yards further, luck aside, and it will be practically out of sensible shotgun range. This gives very little time for a second shot, and once again this demands a completely instinctive shot. The second barrel will only be successful if the eyes remain glued to the target, if the gun keeps moving along the target flight line, and if the shot is fired without any hesitation. There is no time for conscious thought, just follow up the first shot with a well-focussed second. Trust your instincts.

To keep the second barrel up to scratch many, indeed most, Olympic Trap shooters will shoot at any large pieces left intact after their successful first shot. This is important since it maintains good second barrel rhythm, as well as helping the shooter psychologically.

11

SHOOTING PSYCHOLOGY

EW PEOPLE would dispute the fact that the most important requirement for success in any sport is mastery of its basic physical techniques. Only with this mastery can you hope to approach your true potential. Yet once the physical side of your sport is under control, admittedly a process that for even the most talented will take several years of regular practice to achieve, attention to the mental aspect can often transform a good sportsman into a champion. This is well known and understood in many sports, even in other shooting sports, yet in the UK mental preparation has largely been ignored by the clay shooting world.

In the UK there is a lack of qualified instruction in advanced shooting coaching even at the physical level. With this uncertainty over shooting method mental techniques have received little attention. There is even a suspicion among some clay shooters that reliance on mental preparation reveals some sort of weakness: real men do not need psychologists! That is as may be, yet most experienced shooters have, at one time or another, found themselves in a posi-

tion where they should have won and yet they have failed. Has this failure been entirely due to a lack of technical ability? That smooth swing that worked so well through the early part of the shoot suddenly feels as though it is stuck in treacle, the earlier perfect timing inexplicably becomes ragged and unsure. What has happened? The uncharitable will claim that the shooter cracked under the pressure, and although they might well be right such observations are not helpful. Such failures serve only to reinforce the original problem: negative thinking brought about by a lack of self belief.

COMBATING NEGATIVE THINKING

Negative thinking is something we all suffer from in one way or another. This is perfectly natural and even necessary in many aspects of everyday life. Such thinking helps divert us from rash behaviour. For instance, it is a form of negative thinking that prevents an intelligent driver from overtaking another vehicle on a blind bend. The driver does

not know but he strongly suspects that should he make the manoeuvre he would inevitably meet another vehicle coming the other way, and end up in hospital, or dead. In fact, probably three out of five times he would get away with it. Luckily, his life saving negative thinking tells him that these odds are pretty poor. In the same way, concern for personal survival stops most of us making parachute jumps, taking up hang gliding or climbing sheer rock faces. Without indulging in these activities we can still visualize an unpleasant outcome: the parachute failing to open, the hang glider breaking up in the air, the frantic scrambling for a finger hold on the rock face, all followed by long and fatal drops onto the ground far below. These are all examples where negative thinking could be said to have a positive result: our minds keep us out of trouble. Yet this same negative attitude has an annoying habit of arising when it is definitely not required: for instance at job interviews, at important social gatherings, perhaps when giving a speech, and often in the sporting arena. While few such situations are actually life threatening there are other fears from which all of us naturally recoil: the fear of looking foolish, the fear of sounding foolish, the fear of making a social gaff, the fear of failing to live up to expectations. These fears and many others like

them can be neatly encapsulated in the one great fear: the fear of failure. It is ironic that it is this very fear that so often causes failure.

As was mentioned at the beginning of this chapter the most effective way to develop proficiency is to train regularly in the physical techniques. This applies as much to making a good and interesting speech as it does to lifting great weights, running the 10,000 m or successfully shooting clay targets. The ability to perform the task becomes ingrained, almost automatic, and performance standards improve. Despite a high level of technical ability many shooters still find themselves unable to match their competition scores to those they achieve in practice. Such shooters suffer from a lack of self belief. They have a poor image of themselves, can-

48 (Left) *Many shooters like to practice mount and swing immediately before a round. Here Olympic Trap man, Kevin Brennan, prepares himself for the fray. . . .*

49 (Right) *. . . then concentrates on the task between shots*

not see themselves as winners or even good performers, and inevitably fail to perform to a reasonable standard. We have all heard the advice: 'Think positively!' but what exactly does this mean?

The power of positive thinking has been well documented over the years. Simply repeating the chant: 'Every day, in every way, I get better and better' was once portrayed as the ideal way to improve every aspect of a person's life, and there is no doubt it worked for a lot of people. The drawback with this approach was that it failed to focus on anything in particular, and because of this the results tended to be somewhat diluted. Modern methods prefer to concentrate on specifics, which in our case means shooting and its improvement.

VISUALIZATION TECHNIQUES

One of the most effective methods for self improvement is the so-called visualization technique. In this, the shooter uses the power of his imagination to transform his mental attitude from negative self doubt to positive self belief. The effectiveness of this form of mental rehearsal is in direct proportion to the shooter's level of competence. It will have the least effect on the performance of a beginner but should form a vital part of the advanced shooter's training programme. The technique can be used at several levels.

First level

First level is conducted in a state of perfect relaxation, preferably lying flat on your back on the bed in a darkened room. For maximum effect total relaxation is vital. Lie on the bed, feet apart and arms comfortably by your side. Starting with your left foot consciously relax each toe, then the whole foot, then the ankle, knee and thigh muscles. Do the same with the right leg. The same method is used with the fingers, hands and arms, one limb at a time. Then relax the trunk, shoulders and neck. The face must also be fully relaxed, which means the mouth will be slightly open. Breathing should be gentle, concentrated in the abdomen, not the upper chest. Should anything disturb you as

50 *Italian Olympic Trap shot, Marco Conti, on the line. Keeping your mind straight between shots is often the hardest part. Many O/T shooters never watch the targets of the other five squad members*

you are relaxing start the whole process again. When completely relaxed your body, head and limbs will feel heavy, as though sinking into the bed. Do not fall asleep! With practice total relaxation can be achieved quite quickly. In this relaxed state the mind is very receptive to suggestion, the perfect condition in which to practise visualization techniques.

The visualization methods you use must all be positive, and you can give your imagination full rein. For instance, if you are a Skeet shooter you could visualize yourself moving from stand to stand, going through the entire procedure, loading the gun, taking the address position, calling for the singles and doubles, smoothly turning and moving the gun, breaking the target, following through. Most people are surprised to discover that this exercise is a lot more difficult than it would appear. At first the mind jumps all over the place, refusing to hold the required image for more than a few seconds. It is all too easy to find that you are thinking about something else altogether. Do not let your mind get away with it. Drag it back to its task, and gradually with practice focussed concentration will improve. The same technique can be employed equally easily for Trap and Sporting. You can extend this further by visualizing yourself in a shoot-off and, of course, winning it. Pick a worthy opponent, perhaps the current British champion, and visualize yourself beating him, then standing on the podium accepting the cup with a big smile on your face, everyone cheering and clapping.

Second level

The second visualization technique involves the use of the gun. Quite simply, you shoot targets in your mind, this time using the gun on various imaginary shooting stands. The place to do this exercise is in a darkened room, which prevents you learning the bad habit of looking at the barrels. Load the gun with snapcaps, address the imaginary target and shoot it just as you would if it were real, seeing it break. This is an ideal opportunity to perfect your gun mounting, too. This technique allows you to blend the mental and the physical.

Third and fourth levels

The third visualization technique takes place during actual shooting practice. Using the experience of the previous two methods each shot is seen in the mind's eye before the target is called for, a quick mental rehearsal. In effect this gives the shooter the mental equivalent of a practice shot before he commits himself to the real thing. Once the target and the shot can be visualized quickly and clearly this becomes a very powerful mental aid. The fourth visualization technique is simply the third put into action during actual competition. As soon as you can make the method work during practice then it is time to put it to work for you.

There are several important points to observe while putting these techniques into practice. When mentally rehearsing it is essential to maintain in your mind the speed at which the activity would take place. In other words, if you are a Trap shooter, your imaginary round of

Total focus

A good example of total focus occured during an international Skeet event in Italy, during an untypical spell of stormy weather. One of the British competitors, our top junior at the time, walked onto station five, shot both his singles then loaded his gun and settled for the difficult pair. As he called for his targets there was a tremendous flash of lightning that crackled across the horizon right in front of him. He shot the pair perfectly, completed his round (he shot 25 straight) and came off smiling. When questioned as to his lack of reaction to the lightning he seemed taken aback. We were all very impressed when he said, perfectly seriously, that he had seen no lightning. None of us was surprised when he won that junior event with targets to spare!

Trap should take place at the same tempo at which a real round would be shot. If you are rehearsing for a particular event then knowledge of the shooting ground is important. Are there thick dark woods in the background? Is the background mostly open sky? Is it a mixture of trees and sky? Are the targets black/orange/yellow/white? All these factors can be included in your visualization practice.

It is important to maintain all four methods at a good level. Technique one is a vital pure mental exercise, technique two is a blend of physical and mental, technique three is an extension of two and technique four is an extension of three. The four complement one another, and none should be dropped from the programme of improvement. The beauty of it is that it costs absolutely nothing other than time, and yet is highly effective.

CONCENTRATION

'You must concentrate!' This must be one of the most overworked commands in sport, because without an explanation of what this entails the order is meaningless. A word that received much

publicity during the Barcelona Olympic
Games in 1992 was 'focus'. It means
keeping your mind firmly on the job at
hand, not allowing it to stray. It is a
good explanation of what concentration
means. It was easy to spot the focussed
runners prior to each event. When the
television camera went along the line
up, identifying each competitor, the
focussed runners appeared to be in a
different world. They looked right
through the camera, and failed to ac-
knowledge its presence. Those that were
not so committed to the task ahead
smiled at the camera: some even waved

51 *Although Trap shooters seldom watch
other squad members shoot, Sporting shooters
always do! At Sporting everyone shoots exactly
the same targets, so it is a good idea to 'go to
school' on the preceeding shooter, especially if
he is a main contender like Mickey Rouse*

and mouthed greetings to friends and loved ones at home. Needless to say the latter examples were not later standing on the podium for the medal ceremony.

Ritual

A great aid to achieving focus, or concentration, is ritual. This ritual can take many forms, yet all top shooters have their own. There is security in ritual. A round of Skeet or Trap or Sporting does not start as you walk onto the first stand: that is only the physical beginning. The mental beginning, the ritual, starts much earlier, perhaps even as you wake up in the morning. A relaxed breakfast, arriving in plenty of time at

52 *Two shooters staying focussed as Great Britain O/T Team shooter, Ian Peel, goes to work on an ABT target*

the ground, walking along the different stands or ranges observing the shooting, all these things are part of the ritual calculated to get the shooter into a 'ready to shoot' frame of mind. Contrast this steady awakening of the shooter's state of readiness with that of the poorly prepared competitor. He leaps out of bed at the last moment, rushes his breakfast or misses it altogether, arrives at the first stand at the last moment. It is no wonder if he then shoots like an idiot.

A calm approach makes all the difference, and not just prior to the first stand but throughout the event. It is never wise to get involved in story telling or joke sessions just before shooting, either. This arouses the type of excited mental activity that has no place in shooting. Stay away from card games,

too. The totally focussed competitor will become gradually removed from his surroundings as his time to shoot approaches. He will not want any interference with his mental preparation and will almost certainly cut short another's attempts at conversation. His mind is becoming more and more preoccupied with the thought of what's to come.

Retaining focus

Retaining focus when clay shooting is relatively easy during the moments of actually calling for and shooting the targets. The danger to concentration arises during those regular periods between shots when waiting for others to take their turn. At Trap these periods of inactivity can be as much as minute, more for Skeet and some types of Sporting. However you occupy these moments it is vitally important that your mind doesn't wander from its task. There are many different rituals adopted by shooters to help keep themselves focussed. Some will look down at the ground while gently shuffling their feet. Others will stare unseeingly into the far distance. Some constantly adjust their hat or glasses, or fiddle with their shooting jacket. Once it is their turn top shooters will go through exactly the same routine, loading the gun, perhaps adjusting the cartridges in the chamber, taking their stance and then calling for the target. In all cases you could set a stop watch by them from the moment they begin to prepare for the shot up to the time they call for the target. Each individual has his own timing, but it never varies. One leading Italian Trap shooter appears almost

> ### Counting chickens . . .
>
> I learned a salutary lesson very early on in my international career. During a 200 target event in Norway I noticed that many of the foreign shooters, when shooting a perfect 25 straight, would do a little bow to the clapping spectators, or raise their hats in acknowledgement. This sort of thing never happened in the UK, (nor does it now) and I began to think that it was quite a nice gesture. By the final round of the competition I needed to shoot all 25 targets to get into a shoot-off for one of the minor medals. I shot steadily round to station eight, shot the high target then turned to take the low one. As I set myself and called for the target the thought crossed my mind: shall I raise my cap or bow? I was still mentally discussing it with myself when the target flew past untouched by my shot! This was a classic example of poor concentration, or bad focus. It was a hard lesson, but well learned.

agitated when you first watch him in action. He shuffles his feet, adjusts his hat, fiddles with his ears muffs: he is constantly in motion between shots. Yet after watching him for several shots it becomes apparent that he does precisely the same things, in the same order, time after time. After a final fiddle with his ear muffs he closes his gun, mounts it and calls immediately for his target. This is his ritual, and it has helped him take two Olympic Gold medals and a world championship.

Concentration can be lost even when

thinking shooting. You can begin to think about target difficulty, how well others are doing, how easy it would be to shoot the remaining targets quickly and get it over with. All these negative thoughts can cause missed targets. Many shooters prefer to stay away from the score board, believing that to read others' successes could start them thinking negatively. Others get positive encouragement from the scoreboard. You'll soon discover to which camp you belong and act appropriately.

A *word of warning!*

Strangely enough, an insidious train of thought can be prompted by thoughts of winning. With only ten, six or even three targets to go, it is fatal to start thinking that you have got the championship sown up. You might only have to hit one of the last three to win, but you do have to hit it! Relax your concentration and instead start seeing yourself collecting that gold medal and woosh! those targets can get away all too easily.

CONCLUSION – SETTING YOUR GOALS

NYONE WHO claims he competes without a care in the world is either a liar or he is in the wrong sport. Taking part in competition lays it all on the line. There is no hiding place: the truth is certain to come out and you can no longer fool yourself or others as to your prowess! This inevitably means you will feel a certain degree of pressure, and this can affect performance if it isn't kept under control. The psychology of shooting is discussed elsewhere, but there are other factors which must also be considered.

COMPETITION PREPARATION

Clay shooting at the top level requires a high degree of physical fitness. There is little call for hard physical exertion in clay shooting, of course, but only a physically fit person will have the sharp reflexes necessary for good performance. A game that is very complementary to clay shooting is squash. The game requires considerable fitness (or soon establishes it), hones fine reflexes, while the best side effect is the assistance it gives to concentration on the target.

Anyone who can keep a squash ball focussed throughout a game will have no problems with clay targets. Other similarly good games are tennis and badminton.

A good night's sleep is also a prerequisite if you hope to shoot in good condition the next morning. It is amazing how many otherwise intelligent people will go to a shoot and promptly get involved in drinking or card playing sessions, or worse. There are those who indulge in this sort of behaviour who still on occasion manage to shoot very well, but they are mostly notable for the times they shoot like idiots. If you take your shooting seriously keep away from the carousers! If you share a room with someone, and most teams have two to a room, then try to room with someone of similar temperament to yourself. Sharing with someone who likes to talk is actually better than you might imagine. I always used to room with my GB team mate, Jim Sheffield. With the lights out we would natter about technique, other shooters, our own shooting, guns, anything of shooting interest. These conversations seldom

141

lasted more than fifteen minutes because we would soon drift off to sleep!

If you are really hyped for the event, and most serious competitors will be, then getting to sleep the night before the start of the competition can be a problem to some people. Never resort to sleeping pills since these do not grant refreshing sleep: quite the opposite, in fact. Some people find they lay wide awake, shooting targets. This sort of thing can be quite exhausting, of course, and usually you will slip into an uneasy sleep. Do not worry if this happens to you. Most people do it early in their shooting careers and actually will have had a satisfactory night's sleep, even though the next morning they will be convinced they did not sleep a wink. More satisfactory is to fall asleep the moment your head hits the pillow. Practising the relaxation techniques described in Chapter 11 will prove a great aid to a good night's sleep.

For those who find themselves in their national team for the first time, usually away in a foreign country, it can be quite surprising just how low-key an evening with the 'old stagers' tends to be. The following is a typical evening spent by the Great Britain Skeet and Trap team before and during a competition. A relaxed meal in the team hotel might be followed by a casual amble around the local town, with perhaps a coffee (rarely beer) and chat in some pavement café. This leads to further purposeless ambling around which eventually ends up back at the hotel, then a quiet natter and bed by about 10.30. Boring? Yes, very, but that is the whole point. Nobody gets involved in anything that might distract them from their true purpose, which is to shoot as well as possible. Some newcomers to the team, especially juniors, initially treat a trip abroad as a free holiday: they soon learn differently. Once the shoot is over then anything goes, as long as it is legal and does not risk bringing the team into disrepute (the quickest way to end your international career). Funnily enough, though, most sensible shooters keep well away from the night spots even when the pressure is off.

Food can sometimes be a problem when shooting in certain foreign countries. If there is any doubt about the water then steer clear of salads or any uncooked food. Once, when in Mexico City for a World Cup event, nearly 20 per cent of the competitors had badly upset stomachs while one ended up in hospital with severe food poisoning. Those who knew the ropes kept well away from street food and hotel salads and survived for ten days on well-cooked chicken and beef, supplemented with vitamins.

PRACTICE DAYS

All major events permit practice prior to the event, and as many as four days are set aside for this purpose. The best shooters know what they need to do to get the best out of themselves, and just because the opportunity to shoot all day is on offer it is seldom a good idea to take it. If you normally shoot fifty targets twice a week then don't be tempted to shoot 150 over each of the available days. Not only will you tire yourself you will probably leave all your best shooting on the practice ground. It is much more sensible to shoot your usual fifty and then call it a day. Even if you are having problems with a particular target do not make an issue of it by firing off several boxes of cartridges trying to put it right. You will almost certainly make matters worse. The purpose of these pre-shoot sessions is to allow familiarization with target colour, visibility and speed, and background. It is not the time to start learning to shoot! Many of the leading teams shoot just two of the three or four days available, usually leaving the last day out altogether. This allows each team member time to familiarize himself with the targets and background, and leaves a day's rest to prepare for the event proper.

COMPETITION

Once the event begins the competitor is on his own. There might be a team as well as an individual event but shooting is a solitary sport: you cannot blame anyone else if your poor score lets the team down, nor can you seek help during a round or while shooting on a Sporting stand.

First exposure to a major event can be very traumatic. Frequently you will find yourself shooting on a squad full of well known names, perhaps Olympic, World and European champions. Do not be put off! They will be totally absorbed by their own efforts and will not have the time to notice you. Probably, with big reputations to live up to, they will be just as nervous as you are.

One British ISU Skeet shooter, on his first and only outing for his country, found himself on a squad that included two ex-world champions and two ex-European champions! On the last practice day, when the squads were posted, he remarked that his was the only name he had not heard of!

After the first round he was the only one of the six to have missed a target. He suffered through eight rounds over three days, then declared at the end that he would not subject himself to that torture ever again. He claimed that it had been like going to eight funerals, with him as the dead body! Yet, had he known it, none of the other five shooters had even been aware of him. He never shot worse than 22×25, actually managed one 25 straight and finished with a score of 184×200. He was not last in the event, and yet he had psyched himself out of the competition even before the first shot had been fired. Nevertheless, the self imposed misery of it all caused him to withdraw from international shooting, spoiling a potentially fine career.

SET A GOAL

Although it has probably been achieved, it is not realistic to expect to win a major event on your first time out, even if you are a wonderful shot. There will be others, just as good, who have greater experience to draw upon. This counts for a lot. This does not mean you should expect to be last, either, though. At your first big shoot go with an open mind, determined to put into practice everything you have trained for in the preceeding period. Forget the opposition, concentrate and shoot your best.

If you finish in the top half on the results sheet then congratulate yourself.

First time out you have beaten half the best. Wherever you finish, determine that next time you will aim to improve your position by perhaps ten places. Build on this and you will eventually find, if all goes to plan, that you can realistically hope to finish in the top ten at each event. Even for those at the top level this is a fine achievement, and if you can consistently finish in the top ten then sooner or later you will be amongst the medals. Once this happens your confidence will receive a tremendous boost, and many shooters are transformed after winning their first medal. You are suddenly a 'name', someone to worry the opposition whenever you appear. This is the platform from which most winning scores are launched. But be patient: do not set your goals too high. Keep them at a realistic level and build on them.

CLASSIFICATION

FOR ALL but the best shots the classification system is an important aspect of clay shooting, since it enables shooters to compete against those of similar ability rather than having to take on the whole field. It is similar in concept to the golf handicap, although far less complicated. This happy arrangement means that newcomers and average shots do not find themselves having to compete with the current British Champion, so can take part with a better chance of getting among the prizes.

In most countries there are four main classes in each discipline. These are 'A', 'B', 'C', and 'D' for the international events, and 'AA', 'A', 'B', and 'C' for the domestic disciplines. These classifications are based on a shooter's average score over a prescribed period, usually a year. In some countries, notably the USA, a shooter's classification can be adjusted from shoot to shoot. This is very fair since it reflects a shooter's current form which can as easily go down as up, but for most national shooting associations it is both too expensive and too difficult to administer.

The international 'A' class and the domestic 'AA' class are the highest classifications in the UK, but some major shoots abroad will have 'AAA' or 'Master' classifications for the real hotshots, and sometimes an 'E' class at the opposite end of the scale for those who have not yet come to grips with their discipline. Ladies, juniors and veterans also have their own classes, although shooters in these groups are free to compete in the Senior classes if they wish. This latter is not as unusual as might be imagined, and ladies, juniors and veterans have all won major championships outright.

All disciplines have their own championships, and in the UK these are held at county, regional, national and Inter-Home Country level. Any registered shooter may take part in the first three categories, but only individuals selected for teams can take part in the Home Country events. The latter is the highest level to which the shooter of a domestic discipline such as Down the Line, English Sporting or English Skeet may aspire, and competition to make the various teams is intense. There are a lot of shooters in these three disciplines, and making a national team is no easy matter.

INTERNATIONAL EVENTS

International disciplines such as Olympic Trap, FITASC Sporting and ISU Skeet also have their home championships, and winning a national event in any of these disciplines is no mean achievement. But the very top shooters will have their sights set higher than this, and will be looking to make their international team. For these teams there are many Continental championships such as the Pan American, Asian, Far Eastern, Australasian, Caribbean, Malaysian and Nordic, and several more besides, as well as, of course, a European Championship. The shooters from all these continents compete each year in the World event, and every four years at the Olympics. For those countries that qualify there are also the Commonwealth Games, held every four years and two years after each Olympic Games.

The major international events usually have Senior, Junior and Ladies and sometimes Veteran categories but no classes, and medals are awarded only according to the scores achieved. Major FITASC events are usually 'Open', meaning that anyone can enter, but ISU administered events are limited to those in national teams.

ISU events do not have a Veteran class, and at full ISU World and Olympic championships, held every four years and where rifle and pistol disciplines are also featured, there is no Junior category, either. The purpose of this is to limit the number of shooting com-

petitors that take part. When it is explained that of all the thousands of competitors at an Olympic Games only the athletes outnumber the shooters, then no more need be said!

SANDBAGGING

Sandbaggers are those few shooters who deliberately perform badly at a shoot or shoots in order to obtain a lower classification than they would otherwise deserve. For instance an 'A' class shooter might thereby cheat his way into 'B' class, and stand a very good chance the following year of scooping up plenty of prizes and prize money. This despicable practice is made all too easy where classification is done annually. The cheating 'A' class shooter competing in 'B' class shoots well enough through most of the year to win or place regularly, then proceeds to shoot very badly in the last one or two events of the season. This guarantees he stays in 'B'.

There are several ways of preventing this miserable person from profiting from this exercise, however. Computers that work out the averages can highlight or reject scores that bear no relationship to normal performance, thus enabling the association concerned to call the guilty party to account. Also it can be ruled that while it is easy to go up a class it is more difficult to come down. The truth is, while a shooter who normally averages around 75 per cent can easily slip to 60 or 65 per cent at a given shoot, but not to 35–40. Of course we all have off days, but the genuine shooter who achieves a really poor score will invariably throw his scorecard away in disgust, thus preventing it being entered in the computer and affecting his classification. He does not want to be accused of sandbagging!

The vast majority of us strive to improve, and recognition as one of the better shots comes when you make the higher classes in your discipline. Most shooters who have been on the circuit for a few years come to know the sandbaggers, and nowadays shoot organisers and ground owners are being encouraged to report the conduct of these cheats to their respective associations. Their expulsion from the association is the obvious answer, and good riddance to them.

STARTING A SMALL CLUB

L IKE SO many enterprises, running a clay club can be either a joy forever or a millstone around your neck! Most clubs are started by several individuals with ideas of starting the best club in the area. As reality replaces enthusiasm, so this group dwindles in size, until just a few truly keen types are left to do all the work. To avoid this sort of thing it is as well to know from the outset exactly what forming a clay shoot involves. Will it, in fact, be a true club, with a committee and all that this entails, and a paying membership? Will it be a purely commercial exercise, run on commercial lines as a small business? The two are quite different, with different aims, and everyone should be clear from the start what is involved.

Initially, nearly all small clubs operate under the 28 day rule. This allows events to take place a maximum 28 days a year on a given piece of land without the need to seek planning permission. This limit cannot be circumvented by holding more frequent events in separate areas of a five thousand acre estate, for instance. There is nothing to stop you from shooting every weekend for six months a year, though, perhaps from April to October.

Contrary to what many people imagine, the 28 day rule doesn't give *carte blanche* to do what you like. You must obey the laws of the land, carry full employee liability insurance if you employ trappers and scorers, and Third Party insurance if you have any sense. These are readily available from the CPSA's insurers for a very reasonable annual fee. If your turnover is likely to exceed the limit then you must also register for VAT. Failure to do so will eventually bring Customs and Excise down on your head, and you will have to pay hefty back taxes. Noise can also cause problems, more of which later.

SUITABLE LAND

The first major problem when starting a club is also the most basic: finding some land on which to shoot. At first this may seem insurmountable, because unless you happen to know a farmer with some land to spare you cannot even begin. The answer is some carefully placed advertising. Local newspapers and farming magazines are the best bet.

'Land required to rent for clay shooting', accompanied by a telephone number and mailing address, is all you need, and this should be relatively inexpensive. It is also worth approaching land agents, too.

It is likely that you will receive quite a lot of replies: farmers are always looking out for extra cash to supplement their incomes. It is worth following up every lead, too, because some of the best prospects can sound less than promising over the telephone.

There are certain requirements that land for any clay shoot must satisfy. The law states that no firearms shall be discharged within 50 ft of a public right of way. This is not a serious problem. More of a problem is the fact that no shots must be fired which could result in pellets falling on or over a public right of way. The CPSA in their safety rules give a distance of 300 yd as a minimum when firing towards roads and paths. This rule means that shooting on land criss-crossed with footpaths or surrounded with roadways is simply not possible if you are to stay within these guidelines.

If you are fortunate enough to find a footpath-free piece of land then the next factor to consider is any possible noise problem. Put simply, if you start a clay club within a few hundred yards of a housing area do not be surprised if you get complaints. First they will come from the inhabitants, next from the Environmental Health Office. If they decide you are causing a nuisance they have the power to close your shoot. If you are sufficiently thoughtless to plan a shoot this close to housing then you will bring clay shooting into disrepute and you will be deservedly run out of town.

EQUIPMENT

Once you have found your piece of ground it is time to start preparing it for clay shooting. First you will need some traps. There is a tremendous selection available, and it is all too easy to get bogged down in technicalities. The simplest, and therefore cheapest, are the so-called *'flip traps'*. These operate on the over-centre principal. The throwing arm is pulled fully round until it passes centre, when it will stay in the fully cocked position. The clay is then slid into place. To fire the target the arm is pushed back over centre and the spring does the rest. This type, like all manual traps, is available with a single or double arm, the latter allowing two clays to be thrown simultaneously. If there is a drawback to this type of trap it is the element of danger involved in its operation, although this only applies if it is used carelessly.

More technically advanced are the *lever cocked traps*. With these the trapper never touches the throwing arm except when placing the clay in position. The trap is then fired either by pushing forward on the cocking lever or by a separate release lever.

A third and very effective type is the double body trap such as the *'Juba' machine*. This is actually two traps on one mounting, and it allows two quite different targets to be thrown, either simultaneously or one after the other. The lower of the two traps can also be turned on its side to throw rabbit targets, making this trap very versatile indeed. Considering that it is two traps in one it is also relatively inexpensive.

Most manual traps can be supplied fitted to a portable seat mounting. These are ideal where the shooting installation has to be taken away after each event. Where fixed traps are invisaged, ideal mountings are railway sleepers or tree stumps.

The perfect trap, of course, is an **automatic machine**. Carrying up to 400 targets, with cable and sometimes radio release, these traps just need filling up with clays every so often. Less than two seconds after throwing a target these traps have reloaded themselves, ready for the next target. Drawbacks are their weight, vulnerability to thieves and vandals, and high cost. If your club can run to them, though, they are the answer to a clay shoot's prayers. Unless you install them in burglar proof steel boxes take them home with you each night or they will surely walk off.

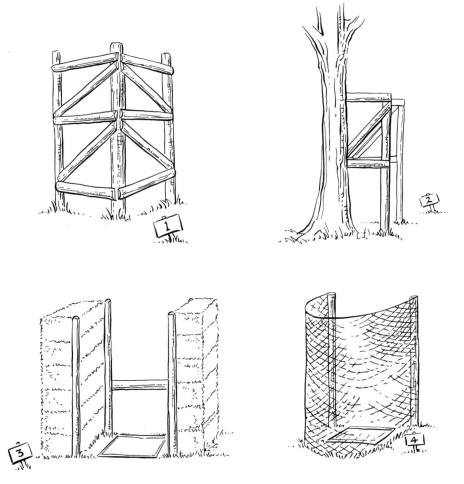

Figs. 21–24 *A variety of cage designs*

SAFETY

'Safety first' is a most important adage when applied to clay shooting. This means safety for trappers, any spectators and, of course, the shooters themselves. Trap and Skeet shooters are never enclosed in cages but do not take chances with your Sporting shoot. Trap and Skeet are well established disciplines, with targets that always fly within certain prescribed limits. Sporting targets, by their very nature, vary from shoot to shoot and from stand to stand. Establish the limits in which a gun can be swung on any stand by using a suitable cage (**figs. 21–24**). These can be constructed in a variety of ways and from all sorts of materials, as the diagrams show. Even 2 in waste pipe can make excellent cages: light in weight and easily transportable these only need anchoring when exposed to strong winds.

Trapper protection (figs. 25–26)

Trapper protection is most important, since trappers are frequently directly in the firing line. There are several ways of making good shot-proof trapper screens: a piece of rusty corrugated iron or a token bale or two are not the answer. The diagrams show some suitable suggestions. Once you have made your trapper screens then you must go and sit behind them and let someone fire both barrels at you. No? You don't fancy the idea? Then go back and build the screen again until you personally feel one hundred per cent safe. Only when you have endured the shooting test should you expect your trappers to trust your protective efforts! Trappers should always be supplied with goggles, earmuffs where appropriate, a safety helmet, also where appropriate (when throwing Springing Teal, for instance), and working gloves. They should also have a red flag on a long pole, to wave when something has gone wrong or they have run out of clays. You do not want them suddenly standing up in full view.

When setting up your shooting stands, do make certain that shooters can move safely between stands. Even if

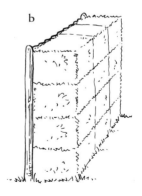

Fig. 25 *The trapper position: (a) corrugated iron, (b) straw bales and corrugated iron*

Fig. 26 *A trench for trapper safety*

53 *When shooting targets going away there is no need for a cage. Note the steel trapper shield, and other shooters roped off from the shooting stand*

ple will have to be paid, and if you decide to hold Open events, involving cash and trophy prizes, then you will need referees, too. Even on the most modest fifty target shoot, involving five shooting stands, this means a minimum of ten staff. Probably not all will be available for each of your events so you will need a pool of fifteen, preferably twenty, from which to draw. Once again, the easiest way to get staff is to advertise in the local newspaper. Do not be surprised if you get a tremendous response!

Training staff and referees

Training your staff is very important. If you do not bother and any are injured then it is entirely your responsibility. Not only that, but if you expect good regular targets to be thrown then it is vital that the trappers know exactly what they are doing. The best method, once you have got in all your replies to your staff advertisement, is to pick a day and assemble as many potential trappers as possible at the ground for a 'teach-in'. Few will have seen a clay target before, fewer still a shotgun. Introduce them to each of the different traps, point out the dangers, show them safe loading methods and how clays should always be kept on the safe side of the trap. With most machines this means on the left side. Let them take turns throwing different types of targets until all are thoroughly familiar with the equipment.

they cannot be shot a clout from a falling clay or large piece can cause serious injury. It is also vital that everyone knows exactly where they can and cannot walk. Rope the walk ways between stands and you should have no problems (53).

STAFF

Once you have established a suitable piece of ground with traps and protection the next stage is to find staff to help you run it. Unless you are very fortunate you will find that these peo-

During this session it is not difficult to pick out those who are willing workers and keen to get involved.

Once your trapping staff know their job the next stage is to train your referees. These might well be drawn from your trapping staff, who can take it in turns refereeing. Explain the basic rules of English Sporting, then give all of them a chance to put it into practice by you shooting some targets. Deliberately miss the odd single and double here and there so that they can call the kills and losses. Missing will come more naturally to some than others. Rules relating to 'no birds' and repeat targets must also be carefully explained, since getting this wrong can make some shooters very hot under the collar!

HOLDING A SHOOT

With your ground, insurances, staff and equipment sorted out you are now ready to hold a shoot. If this is to be an open event then you must advertise it well in advance. With a new ground you cannot advertise too much, although the depth of your pocket will place some limitations as to how far you can go. An advertisement in the leisure section of your local newspaper will attract some shooters, keen to see what this new club has to offer. Best of all, though, is to insert a series of advertisements in the well known clay shooting magazines. Place your initial advertisements at least a month before your first event or you run the risk of having no one show up: there are plenty of other shoots out there, and they have been going much longer than you!

With the advertisements placed it is time to turn your thoughts to the actual targets you intend presenting. It is no good turning up the day before your shoot to plan your layout. Six months later you can get away with this, but those first few shoots will take lots of careful planning. If you are on completely flat ground will you might need some sort of tower to add some extra interest? Can that little pond with bushes and shrubs along one bank be brought into the scheme of things? How about that deep dell which at the moment is full of old farm rubbish? Can a firm trap platform be located in that sturdy oak tree? All these possibilities and many others like them will arise, and few will be solved on Saturday afternoon before your first shoot!

Planning the course

It is obviously important to set the targets to suit the sort of shooter you expect to attend. If it is a members-only club shoot, with a fairly average standard of shooting ability being pretty general, then plenty of easy driven targets is the order of the day, with perhaps the odd crosser thrown in for added interest. If you are planning an Open shoot with cash and trophy prizes, however, then your course must be prepared rather differently. If it is a 50 target shoot, with five stands, then a good ratio is this: two easy stands, two medium stands and one difficult stand. The average shots will get their eights, nines and tens on the easy stands; sixes, sevens and eights on the medium stands and possibly threes, fours and fives on the difficult stand. Your average shooters will then finish with scores in the thirties and low forties, the poorer shooters will still scrape into the twenties, while the hot shots will be looking for high forty scores, or the lot. The worst type of shoot you can lay on is one where all the stands are difficult, particularly if this difficulty is achieved by targets at the very limit of shotgun range. No one will enjoy this, not even the best shots, and if you make a habit of putting on this sort of layout do not be surprised if your numbers dwindle rather rapidly.

Entry fees and exemption certificates
How much you charge for your entries is up to you. Find out what other local clubs charge and try to keep your entries somewhere in this range. Most clubs charge a reduced fee for re-entries, which will encourage extra revenue. If you are intending to sell cartridges remember that you must ask to see shotgun certificates from everyone you sell to. Also bear in mind that non-shotgun certificate holders cannot shoot unless your ground has been granted a police exemption certificate. To gain one of these you will need to write to your county's Chief Officer of Police, requesting exemption. Your ground will duly be inspected by someone from the Firearms Department. They will require a letter from the landowner granting you permission to shoot over his land. They will also want to ensure that your shooting will be conducted safely, and some constabularies have a list of requirements such as cage construction and adequate safety shields that they insist are met before granting exemption. They may also want to know that you carry the necessary insurances, and,

---

Catering

Few small clubs can run to a clubhouse, but a small marquee and hot food is always well received. Catering is an important asset to any shoot. Without the chance of a hamburger and a cup of coffee your shooters will shoot once and then they will probably go elsewhere. Advertise for someone with a mobile catering unit: many of them will be only too willing to come along to feed and water such a keen and captive audience!

---

most of all, that you and your group know what you are doing. Assuming you are granted exemption, and this is not guaranteed, then you are free to give beginner's classes and individual lessons to non-certificate holders.

RUNNING A SUCCESSFUL CLUB

Once your club is up and running then look for improvement. Do not allow yourself to throw the same tired old targets week after week. Vary them constantly or your shooters will lose interest and go elsewhere. Keep your walk ways clear and make sure all your stands are clean and tidy. Nicely painted stand numbers and direction arrows always look better than scrappy bits of paper, too. Proper score cards rather than photocopied bits of paper also add to your club's image. Gun racks are always welcome additions at your shoot:

no one will enjoy leaving a prized gun on the ground, cased or otherwise.

It is often difficult to know why one shoot is regularly packed out with shooters while another nearby struggles to get entries. One thing is certain: the more effort you put into your club the more rewarding it will be. You will soon know if you are getting it right, because no one votes with their feet quicker than clay shooters.

If your club passes the test of time, which means it has survived a year or more without local objections, then going for planning permission to extend your days of operation is a realistic option. Few councils will grant unlimited shooting, however. Probably, if you wish to operate as an occasional club shoot rather than a full time shooting ground, the chance to shoot once a week is all you seek.

Getting this past the council is far more likely than getting seven days a week approval. For most clubs, being able to shoot each weekend and perhaps one afternoon in the week would be their idea of perfection!

GLOSSARY

ABT Automatic Ball Trap

ATA American Trapshooting Association

Bead (Drop) The amount by which the comb of a gun stock is below the rib line

Cast The degree to which a gun stock is offset from dead centre

Choke Constriction near the muzzle that regulates the degree to which the shot charge spreads

CPSA The Clay Pigeon Shooting Association

Discipline Each of the various types of clay shooting, Olympic Skeet, Sporting, Olympic Trap, etc. are considered sufficiently different in character to constitute separate mental and physical challenges or disciplines.

DTL Down the Line, the domestic form of Trap shooting

ISU International Shooting Union (UIT): governing body of all Olympic shooting disciplines; shotgun, pistol & rifle

FITASC Fédération Internationale de Tir Aux Armes Sportives de Chasse, governing body of international sporting clay shooting.

Multichokes Screw-in choke tubes permitting chokes to be changed to suit target conditions

NSSA National Skeet Shooting Association (USA)

Olympic Trap the most testing of the Trap disciplines, as shot in the Olympics

O/U Over and under shotgun, one barrel set above the other

Pattern The width and evenness of distribution of the shot charge after it has left the barrel

Pump Action Single barrel multi-shot gun seldom seen at clay shoots in the UK

Recoil For every action there is an equal and opposite reaction. When a gun is fired the explosion pushes the shot charge forward and the gun back. The 'push back' is the recoil. For a given cartridge the degree of perceived recoil is largely dependent on the weight of the gun: the lighter the gun the more apparent the recoil. Other factors such as stock dimensions and balance also play a part

Rib The top rib on an O/U, Semi-auto or Pump action gun performs no structural function but is an important, though for many an unconscious, aid to accurate shooting. It can come in many forms but the best for most people are between 10 and 12 mm in width, flat, ventilated with either a file cut finish (Beretta style) or centre channel (Browning style)

Sandbagger A cheat who deliberately shoots poorly in a discipline in order to place himself in a low class for the following year

Semi auto Self loading single barrel shotgun, next in popularity to the O/U, though a long way behind

Skeet Short range discipline with domestic and Olympic variants which use the same layout but have quite different target speeds and regulations

Stock On all but the cheapest of guns this is made of walnut. Its dimensions play a major part in a shooter's performance with that gun

Trigger There is just one on any gun intended for serious competition work. Most, though not all, O/Us have a selector to allow either barrel to be fired first

Trap The collective name for a number of clay disciplines, all of which feature targets that fly away from the shooter

Trap Any machine that launches a clay target is called a trap. It can be anything from a simple hand loaded and cocked machine with few moving parts to a sophisticated (and expensive) electric multi-target machine that can be controlled by radio

Universal Trench (or 5 Trap) FITASC international Trap discipline

Wad The plastic, felt or fibre seal between powder and shot charge in a cartridge

SUGGESTED READING LIST

Those titles marked with asterisks are specialist clay target books. The remaining titles have been included in the list because they offer valuable insight into other aspects of shooting and shotguns, or simply because they make good reading.

Bentley, Paul, *Clay Target Shooting*, A&C Black*

Bentley, Paul, *Competitive Clay Target Shooting*

Bidwell, John, *Move, Mount, Shoot*

Braun, Lee, *Trap Shooting*

Braun, Lee, *Skeet Shooting*

Brister, Bob, *Shotgunning, the Art and Science*, Winchester Press

Cradock, Chris, *A Manual of Clay Shooting*, Batsford*

Cradock, Chris, *Cradock on Shotguns*, Batsford

Croft, Peter, *Clay Shooting*, Ward Lock*

Garwood, Gough Thomas, *Shotguns & Cartridges*, A&C Black

Hartman, Barney, *Hartman on Skeet*

Hawker, Col. Peter, *Instructions to Young Shooters*, Ashford Press

Lancaster, Charles, *The Art of Shooting*, Ashford Press

Misseldine, Fred, *Skeet & Trap Shooting*

Reynolds, Mike, *Shooting Made Easy*, Crowood Press*

Stanbury, Percy, *Shotgun Marksmanship*, Stanley Paul

Teasdale Buckell, T.C., *Experts on Guns & Shooting*

INDEX